Witches in the Air

Poetic Essays

Kerry E.B. Black

Printed in the United States of America
First Printing 2026

ISBN: 978-1-948894-49-4

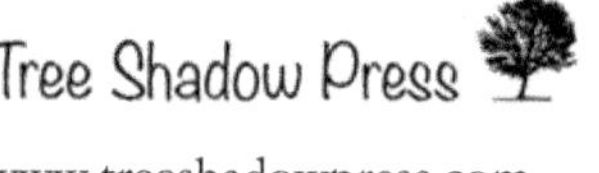

www.treeshadowpress.com

For reproduction permission, contact:

Kerry E. B. Black

https://kerrylizblack.wordpress.com

"Although Witchcraft has been legally abolished, the cult of the witch is so dear to humanity that it is, in some aspects, as prevalent today as it was some centuries ago." T.J. Salmon, 1913

"Why were we taught to fear the witches and not those who burned them alive?" Jacqueline Anne Thompson

"To be a witch is to be a wonder in a dull world." Carrie Anne Noble, *Gingerbread Queen*

"Like others before me, I have the gift of sight, but the truth changes color, depending on the light." *Eve's Bayou*

"When witches don't fight, we burn." *American Horror Story: Coven*

"I think that all women are witches in the sense that a witch is a magical being." Yoko Ono

"You've always had the power, my dear. You just had to learn it yourself." *The Wizard of Oz*, L. Frank Baum

"There's a little witch in all of us!" *Practical Magic* by Alice Hoffmann

Dedicated with love

to all the witches I've known

or wished I knew

or hope to know some day,

and to all who have been falsely accused.

What lies ahead: (Also known as a table of contents)

Insights 198

Dolls for the Deceased

Kitchen Witch

The Left Hand Path

From Within and Beyond

Hedgewitchery

Aunty April

Witchling

Bedecked

May Queen

Bonfires

Wiccan Wheel of the Year

Seasons

Heavens Knows

June

Soupy Spellcraft

NicNevin

Accidental Witchcraft

How Women are Perceived

Threshold

On the Bones of the Sacrificed

Boo Hag

AntiSemitic Association

Brewing Trouble

Homey Things

Witching Hour

Wise Spirit

White Witchery

Black Craft

Tools of the Trade

Kijo

Foxy Ladies

Hidden People

Maiden, Mother, Crone

Weaker Vessel

Braids

Cooking Up Spells

Countercharms

Bath

Island of Witches

Isle of Bakulla

Hellenismos

Appalachian Annie

Granny Magic

When Fog Rolls Down

Signs of a Haunt

Methodology of Protection

Charlemagne

This Thomas Didn't Doubt

Witchcraft Laws in Great Britain

Little Witches, Big Dreams
Magnificent Marvelous
Substitutiary Locomotion
Grandma Witch
Unabashedly Bad
Queen Elora Bane
Hallowitches
Bellflower
Crisis in a Mortar and a Pestle
Witchcraft Through the Ages
Pyewacket's Princess
Oh Snap Snap
Asa Ascended
Mother's Love and Father's Eyes
Children at Play
Harm None
Unexpected Intimacy
Magic in Movement
Bayou Voodoo
Charmed Ones
Unseen Threat
Trio of Trouble
Hazel and the Hare
McDuck's Dime
Music for Mistress
Poor Dead Jane
What Matters
When Witches Would Win
For Good
Nice and Accurate Prophecies
Ties to the Trial
Down the Witches' Road
Magical Music
Lucky 13
Mayfair Magic
Winter Horrors
La Befana
Red Woman
Gracious Generations
Slut Salon
My Favorites from the Wizarding World
Boss Fight
Lighthouse
Wayward
Dahl-ish witches
Can't Do a Little
False Repressed Memories
Magic Girls

Foreword so you're forearmed

Before you begin this journey into the magical realm, please know many of the poems and poetic essays in this collection are inspired by real people and historical happenings. Throughout history, probably right from the beginning, before such thoughts were recorded, humans have longed for (and feared) magic. In many cultures, older people were valued for their wisdom and experience, and "wise women" in particular played important roles in their communities. They provided medical care using herbs and folksy remedies - the precursor to modern pharmacology. In Europe in particular, some served as midwives. Their vision and voice mattered.

Somewhere along the way, the elderly became a burden, and wise women were transformed into witches. Many blame this transformation on zealous Christianity. However, people performed spells and cast countercharms, sought insight into the future, and other magical practices during early recorded history and all through the Christian Middle Ages. At that time, only rarely were the practitioners persecuted. Those who were labeled as "witches" often became legendary even in their own time, respected and valued. Again, they were, with some exceptions, a respected part of society, until a pivotal shift in thinking.

Legislation specifically against witchcraft in England began with the reign of Henry VIII, to be modified by his successors, Elizabeth I and James I. (James' mother, Mary, Queen of Scots, also drafted legal repercussions for practicing witchcraft). James I further fueled the literal fires with his near obsession with witches and witchcraft. He believed he'd ferreted out a coven in Scotland that tried to undo his marriage. He believed through their control of weather, they attempted to prevent his Danish bride from reaching the British Isles. He personally attended many witchcraft trials and wrote a philosophical book on demonography. These legal actions had much to do with the witchcraft trials that held Europe and their colonies in a stranglehold of fear.

The Roman Catholic Empire, meanwhile, declared witchcraft a heresy and created The Inquisition to look into the matters, so many people who faced witchcraft allegations were tried as heretics.

I've tried to bring the stories of these people to life through poetry, to shine a light on the bright and the black spots of humanity. It's only by remembering the past that we're able to prevent atrocities from happening anew in other ages.

However, there are literally thousands of people who have been persecuted for witchcraft throughout time, for most of whom there are no records. A big focus of this collection is on Europe during the 1600s and 1700s, when up to 60,000 people were executed, with tens of thousands more put on trial but escaping with their much-altered lives. As I mentioned, there were witch trials and accusations before this time, and after, but they were much more scattered and exacted nowhere near the devastating toll as the hysteria of the renaissance.

I do look at some interesting, earlier historical cases in this collection, as well, when I found documentation for them.

Also included are some tales from around the world, including ancient witches, goddesses, and folk beliefs. Because I am only an amateur historian with language and geographical restrictions, I don't have every story from every area. However, this is intended to embrace all those falsely accused and all those who were persecuted for their beliefs, too. I'd like to draw a rounded picture for our understanding.

From there, I offer a glimpse into magical workings and some of the ways feminine things have been used to indicate witchery. We imagine a witch flying on a broom or stirring a cauldron. Everyday items, impressed into magical service, some said.

The next section of this collection draws from fictional literary sources I've admired for inspiration. There are some great stories out there, and witches make compelling characters! Be they the villain or a hero, they are intriguing representations of feminine strength. Those included here are but a few, but ones that were particularly meaningful to me in one way or another. Others in this collection found film, television, or music to be their muse. This is by no means a complete or comprehensive list of fictional witchy materials, either. After all, there's more great material being added to the opportunities for source materials every day!

I also understand many people practice a variety of forms of witchcraft to this day. This collection is not intended to dismiss anyone's beliefs, nor is it meant to guide someone to a modern day coven. Most importantly, despite my best efforts, I may have gotten some things wrong, because there are so many variations of witchcraft, filled with nuance. For that, I respectfully apologize in advance. I've done my best with the information I've had.

In truth, this is written with appreciation for what a witch symbolizes and the ways she has been interpreted through art. The unruly, the odd, the strong, and independent. The unabashedly awesome archetype of a powerful female.

And yes, there have been and are male witches, but this book concentrates on the feminine. Since around eighty percent of those historically accused of witchcraft are female, it was an easy task to discover an abundance of stories.

I've also included newer (or future) cases of historical sadness. To this day, witch trials occur around the world. Yes, even in 2026, "witches" are persecuted. The "undesirable" or "nonconforming" parts of societies face consequences, and in some places, are killed. Witch hunts will always exist as long as we continue to push "others" to the outskirts of our acceptance - be they the odd, mumbling homeless person or the Asian citizens inexplicably blamed for a virus allegedly created in the Chinese wet market. Some would say the raids by ICE agents and racial profiling is yet another form.

That's why learning about the witch trials of the past are important. Just as fear and desperation can transform a lonely, old woman into a witch, mob mentality can change otherwise civil people into beasts. Just as people hope to worship (or abstain from worship) as they wish, there needs to be more acceptance and appreciation in the world. And of course, people should be free to express themselves without hurting others and without the fear (or reality) of persecution.

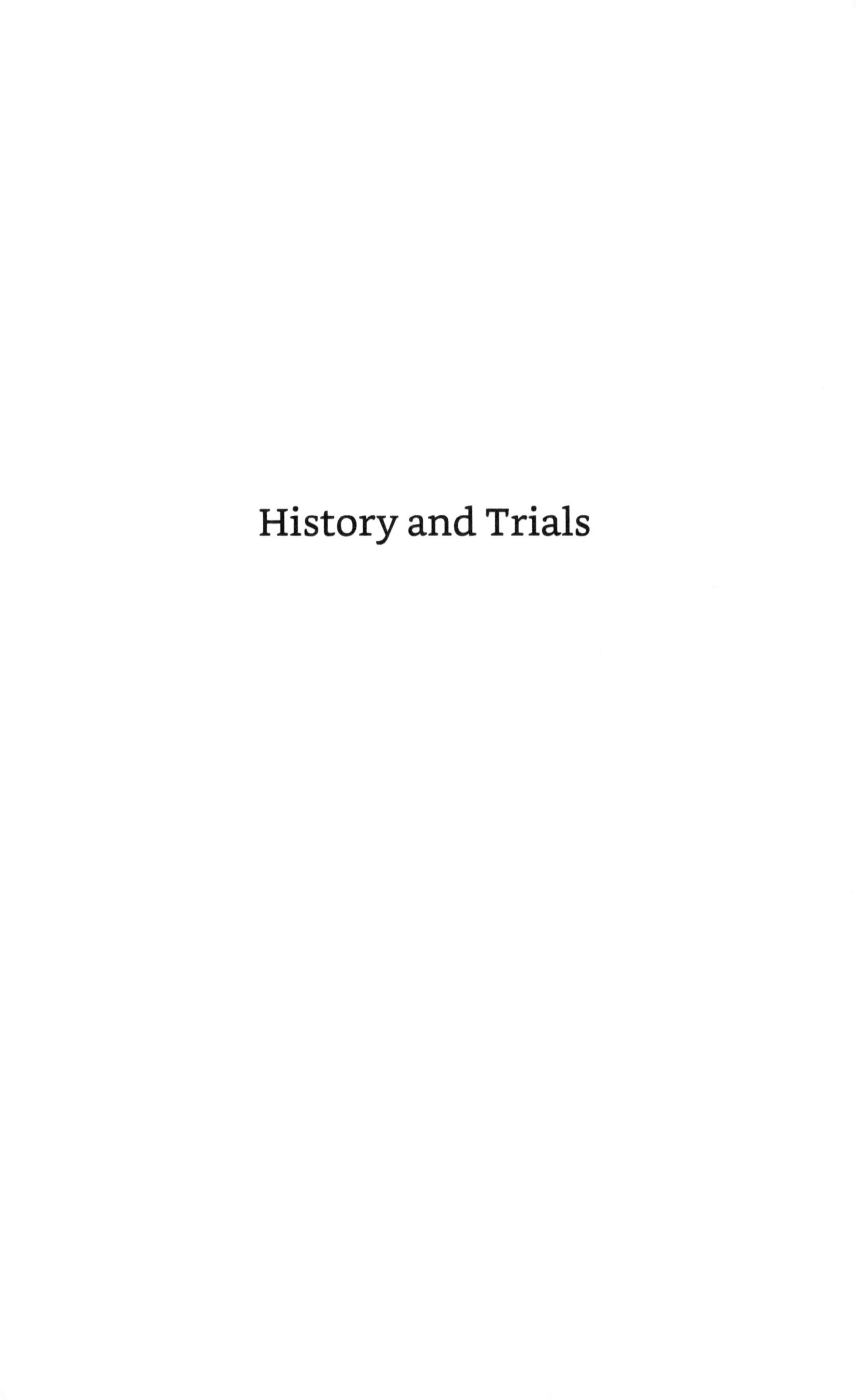

History and Trials

Witches in the Wind

Listen, King, to the whispers
For whistles call forth the wind
To push aside betrothals
And punish those who've sinned

Produce then your evil hammer
Wield it to its wicked ends
Accuse with trembling finger
Conviction to sure death sends

Piled on the pyre like kindling
The lives dispensable tossed
While King commissions a Bible
The meaning within it lost

*About King James I of England, who wrote Daemonologie in 1603
*Heinrich Kramer's Malleus Maleficarum (Translates into "The Hammer of the Witch") and was published in 1486. These are two of many books to blame for much hysteria and death.

Ponder

Imagine how much worse
The plagues would have been
Without the help of women
Who kept cats as companions
Who killed off the rats
Who carried the plague-ridden fleas.

*Historically speaking, women were sometimes blamed for sicknesses, because the "weaker vessel" was more likely to fall prey to dark forces and give in to their sinful natures to become witches with the power to create illness. And grieving, frightened people need scapegoats, even if those lonely, blamed cat-keepers were more of a help than a cause.

Black Widow

Fair of face, she enchanted,
Lured in men by the droves
Married young, soon a widow,
Or so the story goes.

Tried again matrimony
With the self-same result.
Then a third and a fourth man
Her children called a halt

Accused her of murder -
Said she'd poisoned them all -
And worshipped only satan,
The Christian's downfall.

In a trial, elaborated
About evil sacrifice
Yet somehow she escaped
Their infernal device.

*This commemorates Alice Kyteler, the first recorded condemnation for witchcraft in Ireland in the late 1323-1324. She was born an Anglo-Norman noble woman in 1263. Court documents assert she escaped justice and fled to parts unknown. Her Kyteler House still stands and operates as a Public House.

Escape

Where have you flown to, Alice,
With your servant's daughter?
You left your servant to take the fall -
Poor Petronella!

Did you call upon your Robin?
To artful demons sacrifice?
Did you strike a deal to save
Petronilla's daughter?

Did you feel the heat
As she cried out from the pyre?
Did her daughter cry out for
Her Petronella?

*This is also inspired by Alice Kyteler's story, but is dedicated to Petronilla of Meath who was the first woman burned in Ireland, 3 November, 1324. The novel Her Story by Niamh Boyce is based on this incident.

France’s First

Jeanne de Brigue
Controlled a demon
Called Haussibut
Divined the location
Of lost items and
The dastardly thieves
Who stole them
For such services
She was tried as a witch
At Le Chatelet in Paris,
In 1390
Was condemned by
Jean de Folleville
The provost of Paris
To be burned at the
Place du Marche aux Pourceaux
Thus in Paris in 1391 died
France’s first conviction
Jeanne de Brigue

Contrivations

A Fox named Rabiel
Catherine did tell
Was the master of the Sabbath

Victim of Valais
The accusers say
Could transform into werewolf

Tortured confessions
Seized possessions
Imaginative contrivations

*In memory of Catherine Quicquat who was executed by burning in 1448 during the Valais Witch Trials.

Stay of Execution

What caused the accusations?
What cinched the guilty verdict?
As with so many others,
The details are lost to time.
Most intriguing, though I wonder
What caused the overturn
That spared her from the pyre?

*Dorota of Zakrzew was sentenced to be burned for sorcery in 1476, but the verdict was repealed, sparing her the dubious honor of being the first person executed for witchcraft in Poland.
*The actual first confirmed execution for witchcraft in Poland took place in Waliszew on 24 May, 1511, though the name of the unfortunate woman who, through witchcraft, spoiled the beer in the town, was not recorded.

Unfortunate Inspiration

With thirteen other people,
Helena stood accused
Of witchcraft

With wit and common sense,
Helena and her attorneys
Defended against the charge
Of witchcraft

Despite the best attempts of
The prosecution headed by
Papal-appointed Kramer
She was acquitted of all charges
Of witchcraft

*Helena Scheuberin stood trial (and was acquitted of witchcraft allegations) in Innsbruck, Austria, 1485. This trial led to a spiteful Heinrich Kramer writing *Malleus Maleficarum*, in which he strongly suggested no legal representation for the accused, and in fact encouraged the immediate torture of a suspected witch to extract a confession. (This book was published two years later and is still available in print and online in 2026.)

Masca

In Piedmontese

The word for witch

The wily woman

With magic ways

Is a murderous masca

Caterina, it was said

Wished an attendant dead

And with dark arts

Charmingly achieved it

*Caterina Bonivarda was tried by the Inquisitor Vito Beggiani in 1495, when she endured months of torture and was forced to implicate other local women.

Pagan Holdouts

A mix of secular and church courts
Conducted the witch hunts
In the then politically unstable
Italian City-States
Including Val Camonica
Where weather changes from
The "little ice age"
And the resultant famine
Droughts and fires
Plus a bout of plague
Inspired fear and accusations
Particularly of the supposed
Roman pagan holdouts

*In Italy, the Val Camonica witch trials occurred between 1505-1510 and in 1518-1521.
*Most of the documents for the trials were destroyed by order of Bishop Giacinto Gaggia. What survives results from the efforts of Venetian chronicler Marin Sanudo.
*A plaque in Sonico, Brescia, commemorates the suspected over 120 deaths

A Game of Diana

Scandalous sins of the deadly kind
Enjoyed in the rural Italian countryside
Maligning sacred symbols and words
Beneath the watching Diana

*The Mirandola witchcraft trials in the Italian City-States took place between 1522-1525. With sixty tried and ten people executed by burning at the stake, these infamous trials most likely had political motivations.
*After these trials, many individual trials took place, blasphemy for men and witchcraft for women, including the 1588 trial of Caterina Pivia from Concordia, the 1598 trial of Cecilia Pollastri from Cividale, the 1616 trials of Contina from Mortizzuolo and Giulia and Caterina Montanari from Fossa.
*The Mirandola trial inspired the 1523 book Libro Detto Strega O Delle Illusioni del Demonio by Gianfrancesco Pico, which is the first book about witchcraft and demonology in vulgar Latin.

Unnamed Herbalists

Two unnamed women in 1525
Appear in Spanish court records
Accused of acts of maleficence
Arising from their herbalism
These souls were convicted
And their humble belongings
Seized to pay for the wood
And labor used to burn them

Whistle up a wind

Ginger-haired maiden, whistle up a wind
The way your mother taught you
When you were a child
Sing spells of seeing, strengthen hearth and home
Then teach your little daughter
All that you've been shown

Hag Face

Look beyond the visage
Into eternity

Hallowed seeing
Interpretation
Prophetic destiny
Visionary
Soothsayer dreaming
Foretelling what would be

Crafted by a master
The future she will see

*Mother Shipton (born Ursula Southeil) was known as a prophetess in the 1500's. She was the daughter of Agatha Shipton and allegedly the Devil himself. From Yorkshire, England, this woman predicted the great fire of London, plagues, and the execution of Mary, Queen of Scots. Some scholars feel her prophetic accuracy makes her more effective than Nostradamus. She was disfigured, so the less-kind of her acquaintances dubbed her "Hag Face." She died of natural causes and was buried on the outer edges of York in 1561.

Bear No False Witness

Oh, Mother, how frail!
I see your veins beneath
pale skin
And remember tracing
Their path
When but a child.
Cruel fate, this, and vile.
My words will condemn
Not just you but our neighbor
Dear Elizabeth Francis
Who gave us our cat
Whose antics and actions
Brought us such pleasure.
You say my testimony
will save my life,
Spare me from the noose
We three face,
That at eighteen, I should live,
But what guilt-ridden life,
and what will this do to my soul?

*"Mother" Agnes Waterhouse, sometimes called "The First English Witch" was one of the first people executed under the Witchcraft Act of 1562. She died on 29 July, 1566.
*Elizabeth Francis escaped the noose in 1566 by confessing to witchcraft and accusing Agnes Waterhouse and her daughter, Joan Waterhouse (The imagined narrator of this piece.) Unfortunately, Elizabeth's reprieve only lasted thirteen years. She was hanged after a second conviction in 1579, when, in addition to witchery, it was alleged she and Agnes were sisters.
*The first woman executed under the 1562 Act was Elizabeth Lowys of Great Waltham, Essex.

Waking the Dead

Traverse the loam of centuries
blessed cemetery ground
In the midnight hour find gravestones
Widdershins walk thrice around
Wear a stolen vestiment
Until the dead abound

*Lasses Birgitta was the first woman executed for witchcraft in Sweden. She was beheaded in 1550.
*The band Volbeat released a song about her in 2021.

Tormented Life

Tormented by evil spirits since age five
Maria Johan met the Devil at ten
She fell into fits
Met exorcists
Her nephews' witchcraft tales meant her end

*Maria Johan was executed as a witch on 25 October, 1575.
*Her eight- and ten-year-old nephews, who were questioned by the local priest, Pedro de Anocibar, implicated two others besides their aunt. Miguel Zubiri was executed on 28 November, 1575. Maria Xandua's attorney, Pedro Larremendi, requested her case be transferred to the Inquisition, who acquitted her of the charges.
*This case instigated nearby villagers to accuse over fifty additional people of witchcraft, but no additional executions took place since the cases were handled by the Inquisition.

Detection of Damnable Driftes

Hide them away,
Your familiars,
The spirits with the false names.
It will do you no good.
They will find them -
Brought forth by your own son's tongue.

Sing then a song
Of dark vengeance
With children killed in the night.
Darkest deeds brought to bear.
You're convicted -
Just as your mother had been.

*Elleine Smith of Maldon, Essex, was sentenced to death for witchcraft in 1579, along with Elizabeth Francis (from the poem above, "Bear No False Witness") The title of this piece is from a surviving pamphlet from the time, viewable in the British Museum.

Spirits of Old

Assaulted by spirits
From the fay realm
Until at last taken

Alison Pearson
Learned well to heal
From the fine fair folk

Yet suffered did she
Of palsied limbs
In exchange for knowledge

*Alison Pearson was put on trial for witchcraft in Scotland in 1588, confessed in detail about her time in the fairy realm, but denied any contact with the devil. Still, she was hung until unconscious, revived, and then burned alive while tied to a stake.

Weather Witchery

The noble Anne departed
To meet her anxious King
When winds and nasty weather
Changed her course

*When Anne, betrothed to King James of Scotland, was delayed from departing her Copenhagen home by ship because of strange and dangerous weather, witchcraft was suspected. The resultant Copenhagen Witch Trial in Denmark of July, 1590, ended with the execution of seventeen people.

Certain Stigma

There is a Certain Stigma
When it comes to Royal Witchery
The vile accusation
Meant to tarnish the reputation
Of the ladies in question
Before the public and the Lords
It was a way of debasing a royal
And associate her with
The lowliest of the common folk
It was a way to grab properties
And control associates
It silenced political opposition

In North Berwick, 1591

Set the scene of terror
With political unrest
Catholics and Calvinists
Living side by side

A little Ice Age
Causes lots of danger
Famine and fanaticism
Superstition and suspicion

Geillis Duncan the healer
Accused and tortured
Until she created a coven
To destroy the king.

Impoverished Agnes Sampson
Humiliated and tortured
Personally interrogated
By James the then king

With his zealotry
This spurred on a mania
Of accusations and agony
To scar the Scottish lands

*During the North Berwick witch trials of 1590-1592, King James VI believed witches tried to prevent his bride from arriving on Scottish soil. People from East Lothian, Scotland were accused on Halloween night, 1590. Over the two years of the trials, more than 100 people were implicated, including an earl. (Francis Stewart, 5th Earl of Bothwell-high treason) Confessions were extracted by torture in the Old Tollbooth, Edinburgh.

Valentina and the King of Glass

Valentina Visconti
in the late 1300's
Trusted by an ailing,
And insane King Charles
(Whose symptoms calmed
When around Valentina)
Was accused by his bride
A jealous Isobel
of bewitching him
And attempting to poison
His dauphin heir

An Abiding Love

Veronica Desinicka in the 1420's
Enchanted a prince Frederick
And wed him in secret
Which inspired Frederick's father to
Launch the First recorded
Witch trial in Slovenia
Which found accused Veronica
Innocent of all charges
And yet she somehow still was
Drowned in a barrel
And her body holed up
in a castle wall
Before her body was rescued
by her grieving husband
Who gave her a proper burial

The Original Evil Stepmother?

Joan of Navarre in the 1430's
Was a well respected
And entrusted dowager queen
Who was betrayed by new King Henry,
The Fifth of his name,
In the Kingdom of England
Who, to seize her lands and
Holdings and her earthly goods,
accused her of
Practicing witchcraft.
It wasn't until a sickbed
Claimed the dying Henry
That he recanted his accusation
And restored his step-mother

Desire for an Heir

Eleanor Cobham
Duchess of Gloucester,
In the mid 1400's
Consulted astrologers for royal prophecies
Which was proclaimed the
Practicing of
treasonable necromancy.
Further,
She consulted
Margery of Jourdemayne -
Who was known as
The Witch of Eye Next Minster -
To ask for her services
To enchant a desired duke
And at last conceive a child.
For her troubles
Poor Marjorie was
Burned at the stake
And refused a proper burial.
Whereas Eleanor the royal lady
Was divorced and given penance
To walk barefoot
through the filthy streets of London
with a lit candle
(which was the punishment for prostitution)
and after this humiliation
Spent her days imprisoned

Witches with Ambition

Alluring Elizabeth Woodville
Bewitched a man in armor
And the two married
In a secret ceremony.
The man she married
Was Edward IV of England
And Elizabeth became known
As the White Queen.
Elizabeth the White Queen
With her prudent mother
Jacquetta of Luxembourg
Were accused of using sorcery
To ensnare their Edward King
And thereby influence
The workings of the Kingdom.
They were then accused
Of using their witchcraft
To deform Richard their Rival
During the War of the Roses
Lancastrian and York
So did witches play a role
in the rising
Of the Tudor Dynasty

*For folks inspired by historic court life, check out Phillipa Gregory's works.

Doomed Love

Anne Boleyn and Henry VIII
Gave birth to a daughter
Gloriana to be
And not a longed-for heir
Before too long
Anne was again delivered,
But this time to
A heart-breaking, still-born babe
Who was claimed to be deformed
By the Tudor haters
Who also spread the rumor
That the Protestant lady
had a sinister sixth digit
On her dexter hand
Which all indicated
That Henry's second wife
Was without a doubt
an unwholesome witch
And should be beheaded
at the king's pleasure
Which happened on
15 May, 1536
So he could wed his pregnant Jane

Kills with a Smile

The only member of
Swedish Nobility charged
With witchcraft was
Kerstin Gabrielsdotter
Who killed Johan III's
Illegitimate daughter
Lucretia Gyllenheilm
And was suspected of
And convicted for
Her husband's murder
Killed as a witch in 1590

*The motivation for accusing someone for witchcraft varied greatly. Often, the targets of such malice were the powerless, the disenfranchised, those without allies. In the case of royal accusations, or implicating people with assumed political power, however, the motivation was often destruction of reputation and dismantling of their perceived power.

Witch Sisters

Sisters of nine and eleven
Employed by a commissioner
To inspect the mountain folk's eyes
With zeal and without compromise
Discern the Devil's Mark therein

*Navarre witch trials 1525-26 were the first witch trials in Basque country immediately followed by Castilla's.
*The Council of Navarre sent a commissioner to flush out witches.
*He brought two "girl witches" to identify their "kind."
*These trials provoked the intervention of the Spanish Inquisition.
*The Inquisition conquered the Kingdom of Nafarroa in 1525.

Finland's First

Anna, did you bewitch the Finn cattle
To make their milk turn bloody
And the stock sicken and die?
Did you sour the butter that took
So many hours of labor to churn
And turn the meat to wormfood?
What sicknesses did you call down
Upon your neighbors to make them
Drag you through the streets?
What poison did you spew into
The ears and hearts of the young
While practicing your craft?

*The dubious honor of being Finland's first person convicted and executed as a witch belongs to Anna Olavintytar in 1526

In The Shadow of Sweden

An acceptance of folk wisdom
Kept the "wolves at bay"
Until the Swedish church lead
The Finish to their ways
Then Satan entered witchcraft
The trials number seven hundred ten
Resulting in one hundred fifteen deaths
A greater percentage, yet still not the majority, men.

*Preserved documentation lists 710 witch trials in Finland between 1520-1699, resulting in 115 deaths.
*An hysteria broke out in Ostrobothnia from 1674-1678, when 20 women and 2 men were accused of and executed for witchcraft.
*Finland was then often a part of Sweden. Finland didn't see traditional practitioners as devil-involved and frequently gave leniency unless active "maleficence" was involved.

Starving Times

Cold settled on the fields

A blanket of decay

crops rotted and failed

livestock's bones burst

Through thin feeble skin

Dark eyes hungered

Starving times

People ached for food

For hope for community

Feasted on fear of witches

*The Trier, Germany Witch Trials of 1581-1593 boasts one of the largest documented mass executions in Europe during peacetime.

Lucrative Business

A glut of accusations

A tyrant archbishop

Twenty-two villages

With thousands accused

Most all found guilty

The executioner paid

For burning them alive

Made a killing by killing

*In Trier, Germany, the witch hunt lasted from 1581-1593.
*Johann von Schonenberg, archbishop, routed out Protestants, Jews, and "witches."
*Scarcely any accused escaped death.
*The Executioner prospered. He rode a fine horse, dressed like a nobleman, and his wife wore finery.
*The unconfirmed estimate is about 1000 people were killed, with a memorial posted in 2015.

The Salem of Italy

What better course
For a sensible witch to take
Than cause widespread famine
Through child-sacrifice
To the Devil at Cabotina
And thereby starve herself
And all she held dear
While apparently trying
To ruin her neighbors

*The Triora Witch Trials, which are the most documented witch trials in Italy, were held between 1587-1589 and run by the Inquisition.
*Many of the thirty accused women and one man were sentenced to death, but Genoa's Senate intervened.
*Modern-day Triora is known for its witch-themed attractions and festivals.

Witchcraft in Wales

Be it language barriers
Or the cultural divide
Magic didn't present
The same taboo
As in other parts

Cunning folk in Wales
Were not seen as evil
Catholic ideals were
Incorporated
Into magic culture

*Wales reported 37 prosecutions of people for witchcraft. Eight were found guilty, which resulted in five death sentences.
*41 cases were brought to court attention to clear the names of women defamed as witches by other women.

Charming Gwen

Deft fingers construct charms

Weave words into the weft

But when they're widdershins

They deal an evil heft

*In 1594, Gwen ferch Ellis, a 52 years old Welsh linen maker, was the first person in Wales executed under the Witchcraft Act of 1562.

Anie Cat

Anie had a ritual
She used to help her friends
Involving hair and spirits

She was accused of witchcraft
With damning evidence
Her face appeared on a cat

*Anie Tailzeour, also known as Rwna Rowa, was one of 80 people killed during the witch trials on the Orkney Isles between 1594 and 1708. Rwna Rowa died in 1624.

Bien Means Good in English

Wealth and privilege didn't prevent
The accusations leveled
Her many marriages others resented
And pointed murderous fingers
Pregnancy didn't spare her torture
Her husband protested and pleaded
Prosecutors referenced her full form
Until she revealed under torture
She'd slept with the devil to give her a son
Murdered her second husband and
The children he had fathered
For these crimes she was burned at the stake
Presumably with her unborn babe inside her

*Merga Bien is the most known of the victims of the Fulda Witch Trials. She had been married to her husband for fourteen years and was finally pregnant when she was executed in 1603.
*The Fulda, Germany Witch Trials of 1603-1606 resulted in an estimated 250 people executed under orders of the prince-abbot Balthasar von Dernbach.
*A memorial for the victims of the trials was erected in 2008.

Dutch

A dispute over shoe quality
Or maybe over price
A hastily uttered curse was said

A moment of lost temper led to
Witchcraft accusation
Anna confessed to a misdeed

*Seventy-one-year-old Anna Muggen's was the last "witch execution" in Holland. She was strangled, beheaded, and burned on 29 May, 1608.

Caged

Locked in an iron cage
With a dozen cats
A French midwife
Cries for mercy
While people clang
The hideous confinement
With long, metal poles
And men stoke a smoking
Bitter blaze beneath

*In 1609 in France, 600 people were accused of witchcraft, and about 100 were executed.
*Approximately 2000 witchcraft trials were held between 1550 and 1700, but this is only an estimation because the French witch trials were poorly documented, and few records remain.
*There was no national Witchcraft Act in France, so Northern France fell under Parlement of Paris jurisdiction (until 1682)
*In 1682, Louis XIV issued an edict prohibiting the prosecution of witchcraft

Devil of a Party

As teenagers world over do
Maria and her friends snuck out
To attend a party
Never expecting the Devil
Enthroned at the center of all
The noise and partying

*Marie de Ximildegui, a 16-year-old girl living in Basque region between Spain and France, claimed she and her friend, Catalina, encountered the devil at a party between 1606 and 1607.

Rumors and Lies

As in so many trials
Involving witchery
Cases built on control
Though less misogyny
In the Basqueish landscape
Than killing heresy
Where the Pope was involved

Thousands were accused
Interred in tortured jails
Spanish Inquisition
Extracted sins and wails
Presented to the court
Children repeated tales
Fanciful fallacies

One Inquisitioner
Listened with discerning
Dismissed many as false
Applied his great learning
Pardoned those who renounced
Others met with burning
A change was in the air

*The Catholic church labeled as “diabolical and nefarious” the personalized, socio-religious belief system the Basque people tried to incorporate into their practice of Catholicism.

*The Catholic church used the Inquisition to stamp out perceived heresy. Witchcraft was one.

*Between 2-7 thousand people were accused and examined, which amounted to 11,000 pages of testimony. (Recorded by Pierre de Lancre)

*In the Xareta region in 1609-1614, eleven people were put to death.

*Six people in 1610 were burned in effigy after being tortured to death.

*The Inquisitor, Alonso de Salazar y Frias, pardoned people if they renounced evil. He grew skeptical of stories of witchcraft and disproved many allegations. (For example, he asserted there could be no intercourse with the devil if the accused were still virgins) Because of his influence, an attitude of greater tolerance took over, and few witch trials took place in Spanish territories and Catholic lands after 1614.

*The Museo de las brujas de Zugarramurdi preserves the memory of the events.

Toads

They left their warty reputation
To don fine velvet clothes
Danced with every maiden
Drawn to witchcraft

They prepared initiates for sabbat
Called Akalarre in Basque Country
Used words and said ribbit
All for witchcraft

*There were witchcraft cases in the Basque country as far back as 1400's, but those were few and spaced out.
*The court records mention toads - so many toads!

A Quiet Voice Among the Screams

Into Zugarramurdi, Sixteen Ten
Plagued by isolation and fear
Neighbor turned on neighbor
Grudges found their voice
Juan Valle Alverado, an Inquisitor,
Known for his "effectiveness"
Wielding torture as inspiration
Six souls burnt alive and
Five were tortured to death
During "questioning"

With the char of human flesh
And false guilt heavy in the air
Alonsio de Salazar y Frias
Grew skeptical of the confessions
Torture and fear produced
And displayed his doubt
Which brought a pebble to fester
In the conscience and reason
Of self-styled and learned men

*The Caves of Zugarramurdi and their museum are powerful reminders of this dark chapter in history.
*There's a modern tradition to feast by the Cave of Witches on Midsummer's Eve in Modern Basque country.

Pact With Impact

With dinner plate large eyes
And diminutive status
Young Alizon frightened
A peddler passing by

She called upon her Lord
The Dark Man of the Woodlands
To curse the cheap peddler
Who wouldn't give her his pins

The Peddler fell in a swoon
Alizon stood accused
A deluded, poor woman
From impoverished background

Imaginative expansions
To long-held family lore
Included a massive dog
Only Alizon saw

*During the Pendle Witches Trial, Alizon Device confessed she sold her soul to the Devil.
*Her younger sister, 9-year-old Jennet, gave evidence in the Pendle Witch Trial in Lancashire which led to the execution of 10 people, including Alizon and all of her own family.
*In March of 1612, Alizon cursed a peddler who would not give her pins. The peddler collapsed. His son reported the witchcraft incident to Roger Nowell, kicking off the infamous Pendle Witch Trial in Lancashire.

Twice Unlucky

In a lovely French countryside
The sun shining red
Townsfolk accused Inesa
And wished the witch dead

She endured interrogation
Which left her handicapped
She escaped and fled to Spain
But the people there all snapped

Citizens assembled
In the hilly Basque area
And seized again Inesa
A victim of hysteria

*Inesa Gaxen faced the Inquisition in then Catholic France and was found not-guilty of witchcraft. However, she was banished from the area, and her experience under torture left her handicapped. She fled to Spain, only to be put on trial in the Basque country in 1611.

Jennet Device

Be careful, little Jennet,
For what you attest today
Will be echoed in accusations
When you're a woman grown

*Nine-year-old Jennet Device testified against her mother, brother, and other family in 1612 during the infamous Pendle Witch Trial in England.
*Her testimony influenced future witch hunts, since it was the first time a child under the age of fourteen could give testimony. (The courts before this case felt anyone under fourteen was not a credible witness.)
*In November, 1633, Jennet was accused of being a witch by a young boy named Edmund Robinson. The boy later admitted he was lying. Although she was acquitted, she was not allowed to leave Lancaster Castle prison until she paid for her board for the time she spent there on trial.

Witching Country

A tale of two poor, matrilineal families
"Demdike" and "Chattox,"
An infamous Good Friday,
And a precocious little girl,
Nine-year-old Jennet Device,
Saw twelve Pendle people
Arrested for murder by witchcraft

*In 1612, 10 women (including Elizabeth Device, Alison Device, Anne Whittle-Chattox, Anne Redferne, Alice Nutter, Ann Whittle, Jane Bulcock, and Katherine Hewitt) & 2 men (James Device and John Bulcock), were arrested at Pendle Hill, Lancashire, UK. Ten hung at Lancaster Castle's Gallows' Hill, one person, Alice Grey, was accused and found not guilty, and Elizabeth Southerns "Demdike," then over eighty years old, died in Lancaster Castle.

*Thomas Potts kept the court records of the crime and later published a book about the trial called The Wonderfull Discoverie of Witches in the Countie of Lancaster.

*Convicted for witchcraft despite her positive standing in the community, Alice Nutter's grave at St. Mary's Church, Newchurch, with a statue erected by the local community, is where many leave flowers for the executed.
*Pendle Hill, Lancashire, UK, witnessed the most infamous English witch trial in the 17th century.

*A petition to pardon people convicted of witchcraft was circulated by Emma Swinton of the Justice for Witches group amassed over 10,000 signatures in 2024.

Roermond Trials

Mercenaries loitered after war
Dispensing their own "justice"
Drowning accused witches when
The courts proclaimed, "acquitted"
Then came the Roermond Trial
In the Spanish Netherlands
When sixty-four souls died
In A.D. 1613

Italian Infamy

With a toss of a stone
They could cause impotence
A flash of their eyes
Could bring death
They could change their looks
Sicken livestock and make ill
Even the staunches of stomachs
Or so the people of Coredo believed
In their 1614 witch trial

*Maria "la Pillona," Caterina de Fedrizi, Maria di Giacomo Rigotti di Tos, Agata "la Gadenta," Giovanna "la Salada," Barbara 'la Buzata di Coredo, and Anna "la Tuenetta" were burned at the stake as witches in Coredo in November, 1614.

Legend of the Finspang Witches

In Blockula-Hills near the Sorceress Tarn
Phantom screeches of innocence
Echo in the nearby hollowed caves

Pleas unheard by a raging Duke and Queen
Who condemned seven poor women
Pushed from cliff into raging bonfire

*The haunting story of the unusual deaths from the Finspang Witch Trial, Sweden, 1616-1617

Femme Fatale

Seventy-two sorcerous charges
Against a Pomeranian princess
From paralyzing victims to murder
And consulting soothsayers
Yet knowing the future
Said to have sex with Satan
And a familiar cat named Chim
This femme fatale's fortune
Ended when she was named
Seventy-two years old then

*Sidonia von Borcke was executed as a witch in Stettin (now Poland) on 28 September, 1620.
*Elzbieta Cherezinska wrote an award winning book about Sidona titled The Word Spoken.
*Lady Jane Wilde (Oscar's mother) translated a book, Sidonia the Sorceress, by Wilhelm Meinhold which inspired many in the Pre-Raphaelite art movement of the 1800's.

Starry Eyed

Katharina Kepler raised a brilliant son
But her neighbors accused her
Of communing with devils for fun
And poisoning a fellow friend-
And a witch trial was begun.

This seventy-some year old woman
Fought the charges with son's help
Appealed the death sentence given
And won a full acquittal
Then sued for restitution and won!

*Katharina Kepler, mom of the famous astronomer, Johannes, was accused of and convicted of witchcraft in Wertenberg, Germany. She and her son appealed the sentence, and in 6 years of court cases, was acquitted in 1621. She then sued for wrongful imprisonment and earned restitution and cleared her name.

Headless Noblewoman

A cemetery overrun
With talking cats and pigs
Diseases spreading far and wide
A curse'd bridal bed
A member of nobility
Investigated twice

*Christian IV of Denmark introduced a witchcraft law in 1617 which encouraged authorities to investigate and punish all suspected sorcery in the kingdom.
*Christenze Kurkow was decapitated with a sword before her body was burned in May, 1621.
*Before her death, she created a scholarship for poor students known as the "Legatum Decollatae Virginis" or Legacy of the decapitated virgin which continued until the 20th century.

Flying feathers

Dorthe took the shape of a dove
To lead friends on an assault
The other ladies then became
An eagle, a crow, and a swan
To open "wind-knots" and sink a ship
But were thwarted by sailors' prayers
And burned for their wicked plan

Two sisters and a niece of the condemned
One but a girl of eight years old
Incarcerated for questioning
Claimed to have escaped from jail
By transforming into cats
And joining a Christmas witch party
Where Satan played a red violin

*About 140 witch trials were held between 1601-1692 in Norway. 77 women and 14 men burned at the stake between 1662-1663 and 1651-1653.
*The Steilneset Memorial in Vardo, Norway, opened on 23 June, 2011.

Caernarfon

A brother and two sisters
Accustomed to playing games
Ran afoul of the gentry
And though they refuted claims
Were blamed for wicked magic
hung under Acts of King James

*In 1622, Rhydderch ap Evan, Lowri ferch Evan, and Agnes ferch Evan were executed as witches in Wales after a noble's wife died and his daughter fell ill, presumably the work of the siblings.

Terrible Twin Trials

War marched across the land
Laying waste and leveling taxes
Religious conflict pitted man against man
Plague pursued like a wolf pack
Frenzied ravenous for the kill
Mini Ice Age coated crops with killing frost

*Often, turbulent times brought anxiety, and people sought a scapegoat. Fingers pointed to "witches" as the cause of their woes.
*The Wurzburg and Bamberg Witch Trials in Germany, 1626-1631 targeted wealthy as well as poor people, and, especially later in the trials, many accusations were economically motivated.

Torture Techniques

The rack and a maiden met
On a fiery trial basis
Took lime and ice baths
To prepare inevitable questions
Whipped up modification
Of Spanish boots and thumb screws
To make quite a stapada appearance
No dinners or dancing
Flogging melted metal
Before their tortured sparks fly

*Although there's little surviving documentation for the Wurzburg trials, the witch hunts resulted in at least 219 executions in the city center and around 900 around the city. At least 49 children under the age of 12, including some as young as 3, were confirmed as tortured and executed.
*The above were some of the recorded torture techniques used to extract "confessions" in Wurzburg.

Purifying Fires

A man named Martin Luther
Nailed ninety-five theses
To a gothic church door
On Halloween in 1517
Sparking religious revolution
At a time of political unrest
Economic uncertainty
Thirty Years' War
With millions killed
When a killing frost
Sparked purifying fires
For the witches at fault
To cleanse diseased souls
Prevent resurrection
Stop component collection
(for witch's power resides
In her blood and bones -
Her parts make power)

*Wurzburg Witch Trials lasted from 1625 until 1631.
*The Thirty Years' War lasted from 1618 until 1648 and caused between 4-8 million deaths.
*The accusations in Wurzburg started at the lowest rungs of the economic ladder, but climbed into the higher social strata.
*50 Catholic priests were executed as witches during the Wurzburg Trials.
*Folk belief placed great power in the blood, bones, and assorted parts of witches. Burning prevented the collection of such magical components - plus the church believed burning purified the convicted souls, or it provided a foretaste of the Hell that awaited the doomed.

When Whispers Were Witchcraft

It started with a whisper

Talking to herself

Mindless muttering

A suspected spell

*The Bamberg Witch Trials lasted from 1626 until 1632.
*They involved between 900-950 trials, resulting in between 300-900 executions or deaths.

Got Milk?

In a starving time in Sweden
When bones poked through skin
Four desperate women
Transformed into small creatures
To suck the milk from cattle not their own
A man of their acquaintance
Stabbed a knife into a wall
While uttering dark prayers
Until milk dripped from the blade
For him to lick until sated
These five were discovered
By their healthy glow
And beheaded for their witchcraft
And thereafter burned

*Drawn from the limited documentation from the Ramsele Witch Trial in Sweden, 1634

Matrimonial Peril

The pregnant second wife
Of a Bamberg councilor
Found herself imprisoned
For suspected adultery
She knew her predecessor,
The councilor's first wife,
Was executed as a witch
Only two years before
So she seized a chance
Escaped and fled
Only to be caught again
And locked up this time
Suspected her escape
The result of enchantment
Which made her, well, a witch
Her husband entreated
And earned a defense team
With ties to the Spanish royals
So the Bamberg witch hunters
Hurried their trial along
And executed Dorothea
A mere half hour before
The imperial order for
Her release arrived.

*Dorothea Flock was the pregnant second wife of councilor Georg Heinrich Flock.
*She was executed for witchcraft in Bamberg 1630.
*His first wife, Apolonia, was executed for witchcraft in May, 1628.
*Dorothea's plight inspired the formation of the "Hofmann's Friendship" agitation group against witchcraft.

Religious Reformation

Tudor Turmoil sent tremors
Through churches
Throughout the land
Strangling and burning
All in opposition
Of the current change

*The Channel islands Witch Trials in Guernsey and Jersey lasted from 1562-1661 with 66-100 people accused of witchcraft and killed. The first executed was Ann of St. Brelade in Jersey in 1562.

Landsloven

So many tried
So many died
In Norway's witch trials

Norwegian law
Norwegians saw
Illegal torture

Condemned then turned
Condemned then burned
Alive at the stake

*It's estimated 350 people were executed (with 277 documented) for witchcraft in Norway from 1561-1760.
*Laws from the 13th century only punished magic if it resulted in death or injury. That changed in 1584 when King Frederick declared all sorcery would result in the death penalty in Stavanger Bishopric. In 1593, this law was applied to all of Norway.
*The Witchcraft Act remained formally in place in Norway until 1842

Fifteen-year-old Anna

A loving grandmother
Protecting her grandchild
Sweet fifteen-year-old Anna

Mentally disabled
With epilepsy too
Sweet fifteen-year-old Anna

Jealous son-in-law accused
Her of enchanting his child
Sweet fifteen-year-old Anna

The courts forced a witness
Unwilling but confused
Sweet fifteen-year-old Anna

Said her grandma fed snakes
Introduced a strange man
To sweet fifteen-year-old Anna

With no Grandma's protection
They many times exorcised
Sweet fifteen-year-old Anna

*70 year old Elisabeth Plainacher was the only person executed as a witch in Vienna, Austria. She was burned alive on 27 September, 1583, and her ashes were dumped in the Danube River.

Iceland Althing

Rooted in ancestral ways
they made homes in the cold land
With their many Celtic slaves
Seeking religious freedoms

Runic pagan practices
Later included Christians
Galdr/Sadr - Light and dark
Concepts added much later

Witch hunts in Iceland were strange
More men were tried than women
Witchcraft was a part of life
Defined by class and gender

*Witch hunts in Iceland ran from 1625-1683. 170 people were accused. 21 were executed - only one of the executed people was a woman.

Postpartum

She prepared through pregnancy
Knitted little layettes
Agonized over naming
Labored long hard bloody hours
To birth the tiny babe
Caressed the thin pale cheeks
Stared into sickening eyes
Prayed and begged the powers that be
Cried all through the dying nights
Ghost walked through the endless chores
Going on though grieving
Trying again and again
To have the same dire end

*Aagt Germonts, accused of murdering her infants, was the last woman sentenced for witchcraft in the Netherlands. Although originally sentenced to death, the courts commuted her sentence to a stint in the pillory while holding three weighted dolls signifying the three babies she was accused of killing.

Shrinking Hair Horror

A medical misstep
An ineffective remedy
Caused community to
Look at her askance

An affectionate gesture
Ruffle the boy's hair
Pointed to as witchcraft
When the boy's hair "shrank"

*Either the last (or among the last) to be executed for sorcery in the Dutch Republic, Marjorie Arriens met her end by being strangled and beheaded on 18 December, 1591.
*The song "Born for Burning" by Swedish metal band Bathory is dedicated to her.

Death Comes for All

With salves and prayers and drops
Try to heal but fail
Grief to anger hops
The attempt proves fatal
When witchcraft's noose stops

*Margaret ferch Richard of Beaumaris was the last person hanged for witchcraft in Wales. She was executed in 1655.

Transforming Tale

Everyone knew Maggie Osborne from Ayr, Scotland
Who ran the pub for over fifty years
Soured the competition's ale and charmed their wives

It was whispered she could fly
And on her path to Carrick Hill no vegetation grew
Some said she could turn into a beetle
To attend events without anyone else knowing her there

Gossips said a man almost stepped on her
So Maggie ruined him and his whole family
She waited until he forgot to say grace
Then had heavy snow accumulate atop his home
The roof collapsed, killing all there

The man had a son at sea, but not beyond her reach
She raised a storm and sunk his ship
Maggie had a serving girl in her employ at the pub
Who threw hot water to break up a cat fight
The next day at work Maggie bore scorch marks where

The cat who'd been doused would
Maggie was declared a witch and destined for the pyre
The judge ordered pewter plates
Be attached to the shoulders of Maggie's chemise
To hold her to the ground
So she couldn't rise with the smoke to be rescued
By Satan himself

*Maggie Osborne from Ayr, Scotland, who it was said was taught magic by her father, is thought to be from the mid 1600's, but the official records are lost.

Villainous Opportunists

More's the fool who
Sees an opportunity
And doesn't seize it
Or so thought Matthew Hopkins
Who wrote Discovery of Witches
And his assistant John Stearne
Who terrorized East Anglia
As the self-created Witchfinder General
And John Dickson,
Deceitful "Witch Pricker"
Employed in Scotland
To find witch marks
But who was discovered
As a cross-dressing lass
Named Christian Caddell
And deported to Barbados

*From the terrible happenings in 1640's in Manningtree, Essex and 1662 Elgin

Exorcism at Louviers

Orphaned by the age of twelve
Impressed into servitude
Drugged and abused at fourteen
Told she was taken to Sabbaths
Entered a Hospitaller convent at sixteen
There refused to be an Adamite
To her superiors' displeasure
Pursued by the curate Mathurin Picard
With potions and le amour
Until she was impregnated at eighteen
Confessed to marrying the devil Dagon
For whom two men were crucified
Displayed signs of possession
Inquisitors employed when the whole
Of Louviers exhibited signs of hysteria
As Madeleine and other sisters were
Exorcised and the "good" father Boulle
Tortured to extract his confession

*Madeleine Bavent, about whom this is written, was born in Rouen, France in 1607
*An "Adamite" believed people should be nudists, to be as innocent as Adam before the fall
*Father Bosroger published his records of the proceedings in 1652

The Witch of Youghal

A servant, Mary Longdon,
Refused a beggar any meat
Later in the market
The beggar kindly greeted

With a kiss and well wishes
And from that day Mary found
her dreams and days asserted
To beggar Florence she was bound

Flo's accused and thrown prison
Observed by many men
To watch for devils and familiars
And knowledge beyond the ken

From one such captor, David Jones,
Florence tricked and stole a kiss
On the hand through the jail bars
Jones died of magic unresisted

Through the questioning torture
Flo endured suffering vile
The inhumane abuses
Claimed her life before trial

*Inspired by Florence Newton, In County Cork, Ireland, 1661.

Witch's Corner

Janet Cornfoot stood accused
Along with several others
By a sixteen year old boy
Named Patrick Norton

She and the others were tortured
Until they confessed as witches
The others were released
But not poor Janet

Janet escaped but was captured
Dragged to the harbor and bond
Stoned and crushed beneath stones
At Witch's Corner

*Can be found at Pittenweem in Fife, Scotland

Auldearn Ordeal

In a sleepy Highland village,
Auldearn by name,
Our girl Issie told a story
To the most persuasive of men.
What she said would change history.
Of that you can be sure.
She inspired several novels,
Non-fiction mentions, also, 'tis true,
A play, an orchestral piece
And don't forget her namesake,
a slightly disturbing, alt-rock song.
For in April, 1662,
in her coerced confession,
prosecutors leading the way,
She appeared "penitent" of witchery
For all the good that would do.
Her naked skin pricked all over
examined for witchmarks,
Exhaustion bowing her head.
She admitted performing dark arts,
Entering the Devil's own pact,
And attended witches' sabbaths,
As most thus tortured would do.
From there, her imagination
Produced ingenious designs,
Claimed she used frogs and
Rye-meal poppets to perform

Mischievous acts.
She transformed into a jackdaw
And used knot magic to
turn dye black,
Was waited upon with her coven
By spirits dressed in yellow and green,
Who were named Thomas the Fairy,
Pickle Nearest the Wind,
And Over the Dyke With it.
She changed her own name
To Janet
And the Devil gave her his mark
And sucked on her blood
From her shoulder
Before sex played a part.
She described the cloven footfalls
Of the cold antagonist then,
Before sharing remarkable visions
Of the fairies of Downie Hill
And their fearsome 'water bulls.'
She transformed into a crow
To steal from the castles and more,
Followed elf boys, rode straw mounts,
And killed with the flick of her thumb.
Twenty-seven charms unique to her folklore
She used to give aid to the poor.
To preserve her husband's life,
and prove he'd done no wrong,
She claimed on nights when she flew,
She left a broom in the bed

Disguised as herself
To deceive him,
Claimed he never knew
Of her many midnight wanderings.
At least six gruelling weeks
They grilled her
Before holding a trial.
Though no record remains
Of her final demise,
Ninety percent of Scottish accused
Were convicted.
If that were the case,
Before all the townsfolk,
She'd ascend Gallowhill
On the outskirts of Nairn
To be strangled and burned
To ensure no post-mortem
Sorcery could occur,
Yet some say that still
As the dreaded Green Lady
Isobel Gowdie haunts
all the Auldearn Area
to this day and always will.

*Inspired by Isobel Gowdie, "Queen of Witches," a Scottish woman burned as a witch in 1662

Once Upon a Tragic Time

Abducted Swedish children
Led by a scared shepherd girl
Gertrud Svensdotter by name
Taken to Satan's dark mass
Pointed fingers and told tales
Until a tragic "the end"

*The trial in Mora in Dalarna in 1668 ended with 17 people executed for witchcraft and 148 children sentenced to whipping or "running the gauntlet" for participating in a witches' sabbat, even though they were allegedly kidnapped and forced to do so.
*The sensationalized story of child abduction and corruption and the phenomena of witches caused widespread panic throughout the country.

Rapid Fire

Prayers raised from trembling lips
Of those accused of witchcraft
Whipped in chilled winds
On the cold spring morning
Hands clenched in supplication
Knees bent on frosted ground
Eyes upturned to gray, unfeeling skies
While the zealous priest proclaimed
All seventy-one of them guilty
Based on tales of terror told
By the youngest members
Of the tiny village of Torsaker
Of their denied participation in a
Blakulla meadow where dark
Rituals and feasts with the devil
And nightmares and visions
From others in the community
Once tight-knitted as a cap
But unravelled by witch fever and fear-
Though physical torture was not allowed
During the questioning of the accused
Social ostracism and harsh treatment
Imprisonment and psychological warfare
Quickly did the trick
To squelch the presumed magic
Of the Torsaker village witches
Who were beheaded en masse
One after the other, frantic, begging
Pleading, "Please, I'm not a witch!"
Just outside of what once was their home
In the isolated village of Torsaker
Where some were left to dangle

From trees, dripping viscera
From their gaping wounds,
Eyes staring incomprehension eternally
From their discarded heads
Other corpses with their severed heads
Lobbed atop their starved-thin stomachs
Were stacked like so much cordwood
Upon blazing bonfires where,
Fats sizzling and popping
their skin bubbled, singed, charred,
Muscle cracked and peeled away from bone
Burnt to prevent their bodies
from becoming tools of the devil
Wicked witches even after death

To this day, it is said,
On foggy spring mornings
In the early days of June,
the stench of scorched corpse
Revisits those who dwell
In the quiet little village
of Torsaker
A reminder of the pain
And injustices that
Fear and hysteria visits upon
Even the quaintest of places

*During the Torsaker Witch Trials in Sweden, on 1 June, 1675, 71 people (65 women, 6 men) were beheaded and most of their bodies burned to prevent them from becoming further corrupted tools of the devil.
*By 1677, laws preventing witch trials in Sweden were put in place.

Norte y Sur

In Spain, the course witch trials took
Was determined by the region
The Southern areas were influenced by
Moorish philosophy
Without the concept of Satan
Whereas The Foe was known to those
Who in the North belonged
the Inquisition tried Brujas
In sunny Spain, where charges
Varied according to location

Witchcraft and Heresy

The Roman Church saw a parallel
Between heresy and witchcraft
Any deviation of doctrine
Any threat to established order
Any private or public belief
That varied from the approved
From a person once a part of the church

*The Inquisition began during the medieval period and grew during the early modern period. They were called in to question and tried heretics and witches.
*The horrible book, Directorium Inquisitorum by Nicholas Eymerich, appointed Inquisitor General of Aragon in 1357, used seized sorcerous materials to inform readers.

Eichstatt

Burning candles

Cauldron brews

Chanted prayers

Spells peruse

*In Eichstätt, Bavaria, Germany, waves of witchcraft trials took place between 1532-1723.
*At least 283 people were executed (253 women & 30 men)
*The trouble started with 2 troublesome women in 1532, then another rebellious woman in 1535.
*Margreth Auerhamerin was expelled from the bishopric in 1551 as she did not confess to any of the witchcraft she was accused of.
*1560-1590, 24 women were imprisoned as witches; 23 were executed, and 1 was released.
*1603-1612, 20 women were executed as witches.
*224 people (197 women, 27 men) were executed for witchcraft between 1613-1630.
*In 1705, a fifteen-year-old boy called Balthasar Gorck was sentenced to death as a witch.
*The last victim of these witchcraft trials was a pauper girl of about 22 years old killed on November 22, 1723.

Grieving Ears

Midnight storms swirl
Through community fears
Stirring superstition's score
Poured into grieving ears
Recasting societal outsiders
Ancestral agony hears

*The Ellwangen Witch Trials took place in 1588 where approximately twenty people were executed and then again between 1611 until 1618 which resulted in the loss of 430 lives.

Mother to a Wizard

Mother
What economic tortures
Did you endure
To teach your son to beg
And trick and connive?
Mother
What parental tortures
Did you endure
To watch your son's violence
Engulf his every action?
Mother
What corporeal tortures
Did you endure
When arrested to out
Your son's Satanic pact?
Mother
What personal tortures
Did you endure
At your sentencing when
You learned your partner would die, too?
Mother
What physical tortures
Did you endure
When your death sentence was
Publicly enacted - no son in sight?

*Barbara Kollerin was declared a beggar and a witch in Salzburg, Austria in 1675. Under torture, she implicated her twenty-year-old son, Jakob, as having made a pact with Satan to become the magician Jackls. This kicked off the Zaubererjackl and Witch Trials of 1675-1690. 198 people were accused and arrested and 139 killed (113 of whom were homeless. 92 were under the age of 21. The youngest was 10.) Jakob was never arrested or even "seen."

The Great Noise

Shadows cast by fires
Burning those accused as witches
Engulfed great swaths of Sweden
With suffocating fears

*The Swedish Witch Hunts of 1668 until 1676, called "The Great Noise," resulted in almost 300 executions.

Blazing Gory

Brighter than the Aurora Borealis
Flames lighten flaxen hair
Lick at labored skin
Stretched over a silent stomach
That birthed accusers
Who marvel at her silence

*Malin Matsdotter was one of the last people executed for witchcraft in Stockholm during the Great Noise in Sweden (1668-1676). Her daughters were her accusers. Because she maintained her innocence, she was also one of the only convicts burned alive in the country. Reportedly, she never screamed or cried out, even as the flames devoured her.

*In 2024, a commemorative herb garden was opened in Stockholm by local witches in remembrance of those lost to the Great Noise.

Katarina Witch Trials

The Great Noise finally silenced
In Katarina Parish
When men on the Commission
Questioned

The rights of accused witches
The confessions torture-bought
Children as the witnesses
Questioned

One child witness admitted
That he lied before the court
All child witnesses then were
Questioned

All admitted that they lied
Children charged with perjury
When the court and commission
Questioned

*Eric Noraeus and Urban Hiarne and others on the Witchcraft Commission questioned the veracity of the system. In 1677, the government ordered the clergy nationwide to stop all witch panic activities and conduct prayers of gratitude that “witches had been banned” from the Kingdom of Sweden.

*While witchcraft cases occasionally appeared in the late 17th and early 18th centuries, they were isolated, and guilty verdicts were usually commuted to lesser punishments.

Hexen Berg

Ice crystals collect like misspent tears
Gathering sympathy through the years
Beyond, between, after the fires
Tossed those called witch upon pyres
From their far flung scattered ash
The soil secures a fertile cache

*Hexen Berg means witch mountain. It looms over Winningen, Germany, and is home to the Weinhex (wine witch) vineyard and hiking paths.

Burning Accusations

The list of your offenses
Outnumbered the marks
They proclaimed showed
Your true nature
They alleged you met
The devil in the shape of
A black dog named Frequette
At the sabbat celebrations
When you cast spells on
Women and cattle but
Especially against children
Torture caused your confession
Torture forced you to accuse
Others, even your cousin Jeanne
Torturous the end you met
Bound and burned

*Inspired by Peronne Goguillon, who is referred to as one of the last women executed for witchcraft in France on 29 May, 1679. The women Peronne accused included Jeanne Goguillon and Marie-Anne Dufosset who were burned 3 July, 1679.

Poison

Slipped in teacups, dropped in drinks
Tablets to the bottom sink
Mixed and measured, ground and fine
Herbs into food's grand design
Poured on fabric, laced to lick
Poisons more than make them sick

*Inspired by "La Voisin," or Catherine Monvoisin, who was a Parisian midwife and part of the "Affaire des poisons," a cult that poisoned many members of the French aristocracy. She was accused of witchcraft and necromancy in the 17th century after she was asked to kill King Louis XIV by his mistress, Madame de Montespan, to punish him for his infidelity. La Voisin was publicly burned in 1680.

The Bideford Three

The man in black

tempted, tempted

With influence great

Three

*For Temperance Lloyd, Mary Trembles, and Susannah Edwards, from Devon, who were some of the last people executed as witches in England in August, 1682. A plaque on the wall of Rougemont Castle in Exeter commemorates their deaths.

Polish Hocus Pocus

With pins and infant potions
Impotency they prolonged
Bloodletting and bravado
Brought bad harvests and fouled foods
Spellcraft sickened several
Livestock languished long
Polish potions flying further and longer

*Polish witch trials were conducted by secular courts, clerical courts, and by private courts on noble estates, despite many laws passed to prevent such trials.
*During the 16th and the first half of the 17th centuries, 49 women and 19 men were condemned in Poland for using witchcraft.
*Between 1624 - 1730, 116 women and 5 men were executed for witchcraft in Poland.
*The last witch trial in independent Poland was outside Poznan in 1793 when two unnamed women were executed for using witchcraft to sicken livestock.

Fickle Familiar

She renounced her baptism
Spat upon religion
To embrace Satan
And accept the special gift
Of magic use aided by
Her personal demon Knut
Who did nothing to protect her
From witchcraft accusations
Or even show itself -
As if it weren't there at all

*Johanne Nielsdatter was the last person executed for practicing witchcraft in Norway in 1695. She was burned.
*The penultimate victim of witch burning in Norway was Lisbet Nypan, whose life and 1670 death was made famous by Torbjorn Prestvik's novel. She's memorialized by a statue, and a road is named after her.

Beware Who Comes Upon Ye

Elderly widow woman of Fife
Accused by a madwoman's cry
"Beware lest Lilias Adie come upon ye!"
A second proclaimed she came at night
To torment and bring bad dreams.
Confessed then did Lilas
"Since the second burning
Of the Fife Witches,"
She'd renounced her good vows
And belonged entire to the devil
Who wore ever a bonnet upon his horned head
And asked that his maids entice others
To his dark service, in their coven
On the moonless gatherings.
This weary, old soul died
Before those in charge
Could hang and burn her alive.
They tossed her body in a box
Beneath a stone slab
on unconsecrated ground
Between the high and low tide zone
In Thoryburn Bay.
In 1852, people exhumed
The poor woman's body.
They parted her out as souvenirs.

*Lilias Adie (1640-1704) resisted accusing others, though under torture, she did give a few local women's names as witches. She has a plaque commemorating her life in Fife, Scotland. In 2019, forensics artists used photographs of her lost skull to recreate Lilias' features.

The Laird's Daughter

A parent's fear
When one held dear
Reacts in startling ways
Baying and tears
spellcraft appears
Those accused are who then pays

*The Paisley Witch Trial of 1697 began when a ten-year-old girl, Christian Shaw, had fits and convulsions said to be caused by malignant magic of seven people. Five were hanged and burned on 10 June, 1697, their remains buried under a horseshoe at the crossroads.
*A memorial and what's believed to be the horseshoe stands at the site.

Soot Witch

Gossip twists and turns truths
And
Hearts against each other

A servant known for healing
Is
Forced to beg when fired

With seeds that led to silence
Then
That employer was cursed

Since gossip caused job's end
Then
How fitting a response

*Anna Eriksdottir, who was fired by the local vicar when he heard rumors of her witchcraft, confessed to a long list of witchy acts. Despite an appeal to the king by the High Court to spare her life because she was "old and confused" and "full of wild imaginings," she was decapitated and the last person executed for witchcraft in Sweden on 15 June, 1704

Smoke and Silence

Sin weighs heavy on an unshriven soul
Eighty years of confusion
Born into a family of witches
All easily insulted
Denied tobacco at the meal's end time
Gave a stroke to the neighbor
Fired by the vicar for her healing skills
Sowed seeds to steal his voice then
When arrested at the age of eighty
Confessed before beheaded

*Also in honor of 80-year-old Anna Eriksdotter who was the last person killed as a witch in Sweden in 1704.

Wailing of the Wronged

Lay a penny on the cold stone
In memory of the wronged
Light a candle and say a prayer
With a tune sing along
To the wailing of the wronged

*In memory of Marion Lillie, the "Rigwoodie Witch," who it is said was burned at the Witches Stone in Spott, East Lothian, Scotland in 1705. Rigwoodie in Scottish means thin or bony. Folk artists Richard Klein and Karen Deitz and poets David Carnegie and Carey Douglas wrote songs about her, and Ruth Gilchrist also wrote a poem in her honor.

The Islandmagee Witch Trials

Mary Dunbar, older teen
Exhibited acts obscene
Vomited buttons and wool
Blasphemed, threw knives and stools
Showed some signs of possession
Or demonic obsession
Accused eight local women
Had them thrown in prison
Claimed attacked in spectral form
A mob was thereby born
Whose attack before they'd tried
Caused one "witch" to lose an eye
The women found guilty- alas
Mary Dunbar was still harassed
Blamed Liz Sellor's husband then
Mary died - he was seized by men
And convicted like his wife
Though it likely cost his life

*The accused women were Janet Carson, Janet Latimer, Janet Main, Janet Millar, Margaret Mitchell, Catherine McCalmond, Janet Liston, and Elizabeth Sellor. They were tried in March. Although no official record survives, it is suspected the women spent time in the pillory for causing injury; it is supposed William Sellor would have been killed.
*Islandmagee Witch trials of 1711 are believed to be the last witch trials in Ireland.
*A memorial to the trials can be visited at the Gobbins Visitor Center.
*The events have inspired a 2014 novel by Martina Devlin (who proposed the memorial) and a 2023 graphic novel by David Campbell

The Emerald Isle

Ireland is different
Than its sister countries
There the old ways still hold sway

In Ireland they know
To avoid fairy forts
and gave the world Halloween

Perhaps it's in the green
Or the sacred hawthorns
It didn't demonize magic

*Ireland held four recorded witchcraft trials.
*However, there was the "changeling" murder of Bridget Cleary in February, 1869, wherein poor Bridget's husband, her father, and other men in her community believed she'd been captured by the fairies and replaced with a fairy replica that resembled Bridget. To have the real woman restored and the changeling that took her place removed, these men gave her poisoned brews and burned her to death.

Order Pot

Atop a bottomless pond
In the Elgin area
Modern people placed
A memorial marking
Where suspected witches
Were subjected to the
Swimming test
Where bound suspects
Were tossed into water
With the belief that
Water rejects those
Who reject their baptism
Leaving a witch to float
Which indicates guilt
While innocent people
Usually drowned
But could be buried
In hallowed ground

*The people of Elgin filled in the "bottomless pond" in 1881 and erected a memorial to the over 300 trials and the 40 executed in Elgin, Scotland.

Jilted lover

Broken promises
Stolen heart
From a lady
Wily and smart

Foolish man
On wedding night
To another
Received a fright

In nuptial bedding
To give him fits
Bag with ashes,
hair, and nail bits

For this "prank"
She was condemned
For use of witchcraft
Burned in the end

*For Brigitte Haldorsdatter who was the last person confirmed as executed as a witch in Norway, 1715.
*Witchcraft was formally a crime in Norway until 1842

Wedding Curse

Ashes of the promised love
from your poisoned pen
The snip of hair you gave to me
Declaring you were mine
Fingernails broken when
Our passion glowed like blushes
Sprinkled on the bedsheets
On your wedding evening rushes

*In 1715, Brigitte Haldorsdatter was the last person in Norway to be found guilty of witchcraft.

*There were other witchcraft trials in Norway after Brigitte, but she's the last one found guilty.

Poor Janet Horne

Poor Janet Horne
Bore the scorn
Of many of her neighbors

They said that she
Made into a pony
Her only living daughter

So she might go
To the witch's show
And kiss her Devilish master

*"Janet Horne" was the last person to be legally executed for witchcraft in the British Isles. Her actual name is lost to posterity, since Janet or Jenny's a generic name for witches in the north of Scotland at the time of her murder.
*A "witch's stone" in Littletown, Dornoch, Scotland, marks where she was coated with tar and burned alive (1722 or 1727)
*Her daughter, who bore some defects in her extremities, was also convicted of witchcraft but escaped.
*Janet Horne is the subject of the play The Last Witch by Rona Munroe (2009) and the novel The Last Witch of Scotland by Philip Paris.
*Scotland killed around 2500 people as witches during their trials.

Royal Bell

Death came for Bell
Who sat alone
In her humble, Scottish hut
No herring caught
Fishermen fresh
As was her daily habit
In youthful times
When fishermen
Gave fish for special blessings
"Give rich, get rich"
Bell always said
While accepting charity
They called her witch
And never crossed
Fearful of her canny spells
No cup of tea
Future predicted
Her mental slipping ailment
They locked her up
But she escaped
To die on her own terms

*In Scotland, there are three famous witches named Bell. Bell Royal was one.
*Nicneven is the Scottish word for witch or fairy

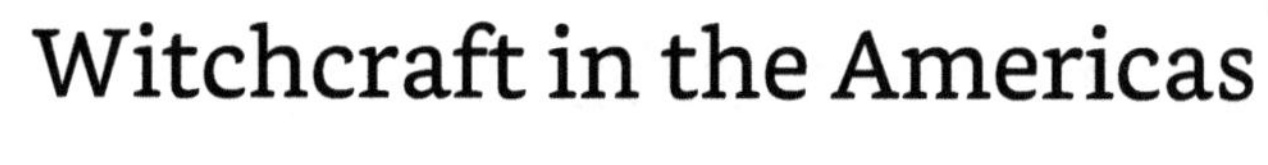
Witchcraft in the Americas

Rebellion and Revenge

Maria bit back anger
When she applied a poultice
To tenderize the bruises
And cuts

Her dark eyes flashed
Rebellion and revenge

Powdered herbs to poison
An abusive husband
Maria gave Lucia
Her daughter

Their dark eyes flashed
Rebellion and revenge

Authorities declared
Maria a bruja
Lost in record keeping
Is Maria's fated end

But

Her dark eyes flashed
Rebellion and revenge

*In honor of Maria de Zamora, an indigenous Mexican woman who lived in San Gabriel, New Mexico, in 1607. Maria de Zamora was arrested and tried for witchcraft. The saddest part of the proceedings is her daughter, Lucia, who she was trying to help, gave evidence against her mother.

Lefty

Cunning and foretelling
Medical mystique
Counter-charm concocting
Left handed wife
Stopped a "spectral hand"
Predicted many deaths
Accused as a witch
Yet her fate's unknown

*Joan Wright was a "cunning woman" who was blamed for using witchcraft to cause bad hunting, baby deaths, and when her prognostications came true, of causing the deaths she predicted. She was tried in the Virginia Colony in 1626.

Virginia

Inflated accusations

Noone on her side

Crops were failing

People wailing

Then an infant died

*The Virginia courts, much more secular in their focus than their New England counterparts, required irrefutable evidence before convicting someone of witchcraft.
*Though court records indicate the use of corporal punishment for crimes such as theft, no evidence exists that anyone was ever executed for witchcraft in the Virginia Colony. However, the surviving records fail to indicate the fate of accused witches such as Joan Wright in 1626.
*The VA Colony passed a law in 1655 punishing false accusations of witchcraft, with the possible penalty of one thousand pounds of tobacco per false accusation.

Young Death

Spring winds brought flu
To the colony
Of Connecticut
In 1647
Spring winds blew
A captive Alse
To the Meeting House
For her witchcraft trial
Spring winds blew around
Her limp, dead form
As it hung
From the gallows

*Written in remembrance of Alse Young, the first woman to be executed in the American colonies. She was thirty-one or thirty-two years old when publicly hung in Hartford, Connecticut, on 26 May, 1647.
*Her daughter, Alice Beamon, was also convicted as a witch in the 1670's but not killed.

Goody Bassett

She fled Hartford, Connecticut
When her friend Alse hung
To make a suspicion-free home
In lovely Stratford instead
Only to be accused and tried
For witchcraft in 1651
On the way to the gallows
She broke free and tearful,
clutched a rock

*Although scholars don't know her first name ("Goody" was an honorarium or title for a woman at the time), the Stratford Historical Society asked local authorities to exonerate this accused woman. However, there's a complication, in that there are few records of Goodwife Bassett's trial, so there's no evidence to review. Further, some feel modern governments should defer to the standards of the day and defer to the authorities in charge at the time. Those authorities were the British.
*15 May was proclaimed Goody Bassett Day in Hartford by the mayor. The Hartford Historical Society hosts an annual Goody Bassett Ball, and a tribute plaque was erected in town. There's even a downtown ice cream shoppe that bears her name.

Watching

In the clear light of day
A little imp came
To suckle witch's blood
From accused Margaret
Who sat knotted for "Watching"

She possessed clear vision
Futures she foretold
Her mighty medicine
Had healed many
But sickened even more

In the clear light of day
A Hellish imp came
To suckle Margaret's blood
Or so reports say
From those who stayed for "Watching"

*In honor of thirty-five-year-old Margaret Jones, midwife, who was the first person hung for witchcraft in the Massachusetts Bay Colony in Boston, Massachusetts (and the second - after Alse Young - convicted as a witch in New England.)
*from 1647-1688, Eighty people were accused of witchcraft in New England. Of those accused, between nine and eighteen, including Margaret Jones and Alse Young, were hung as witches.
* "Watching" was a practice described by Englishman Matthew Hopkins in his witch-hunting manual where the accused is forced into a cross-legged position for a whole day and scrutinized for impish encroachers - any small creature would do, even insects!

Connecticut Crimes

In the English Colony
Of Connecticut
Sickness gripped the land
Children died in clusters

Fearful people pointed fingers
At neighbors and friends
Hoping to stop death with
Allegations of witchcraft

*Connecticut Witch Trials occurred from 1647-1663, with 37 tried cases and 11 executions
*On 26 May, 2023, the people who were found guilty of witchcraft had their reputations cleared by the legislature, thanks to the efforts of the Connecticut Witch Trial Exoneration Project in Windsor, CT.
*A memorial was erected on the site of the old meeting house where the trials took place.

Charity of London

Storm-tossed and ever seeking
Some solace for their days
The Charity of London
Reverted to mob ways

Accused a maid name Mary
Of causing them mischief
Found upon her the witchmark
And hung her until stiff.

*Named for the ship meant to give safe passage to Mary Lee, a would-be Maryland colonist, lynched during her passage on 23 June, 1654

Golden Ghost Girl

Curled on the prison floor
Clothes loose around thin frame
Every inch violated
Every part investigated
With exacting vigor
Starving, dehydrated,
Surrounded by defecation
Exhausted, demoralized
Aching, confused
When a glowing girl appeared
A child in rare golden beams
Slanting through jail bars
Embraced her, then vanished
A spectral vision observed
By ogling deputies and others
Intent on witches' demise

*On 15 June, 1648, 35-year-old midwife Margaret Jones was the first person to be executed for practicing witchcraft in the Massachusetts Bay Colony, which makes her the second person in New England (after Alse Young in 1647).
*Her husband was also arrested, but he was not found guilty of witchcraft. He tried to flee on a ship called "Welcome," but the ship had trouble which the captain blamed on him. He was re-arrested. The ship left. He was again freed from prison.
*Prior to the infamous Salem Witch Trials of 1692-1693, at least nine women were hanged as witches in Massachusetts Bay.

Satan in the Settlement

Tangled forests
Creeping fog
Crops dying on the vine
Solar visions
Native wars
Insects in the food stores
Cattle perish
Freakish births
Witchcraft in the Old World
Nearby murders
Witches hung
Atmosphere turns toxic
Writhing sickness
Bloody milk
Ghost ships in the harbor
Nightly Terrors
Marsh Fever
Evil wore a friend's face

*Mary Reed left Wales for New England. In Springfield, Massachusetts, she married Hugh Parsons and had children, but it was reportedly not a contented home. When rumors of witchcraft trials in Europe reached New England, and women in nearby villages were hung as witches, financial downturns and illness held the Parsons in a stranglehold. Mary leveled witchcraft allegations against her husband. He turned the tables and accused her. The court decided. Mary was killed in the 1650's.

*In a strange historical twist, another woman named Mary Parsons was accused of witchcraft in Springfield, Massachusetts in 1674-1675, but, although she was acquitted, her relationship with her neighbors remained contentious.

Stormy Passage

Storms rolled in
With steely gray skies
The sort that brewed
In scared sailor's eyes
Katherine Grady
An elderly maid
Was blamed for all
With her life she paid

*Like Mary Lee in the above poetic essay, Katherine Grady was also lynched for suspected witchcraft while on her way to a new home in Virginia in 1654.

Gardens and Garlic

Live a waking nightmare
Shiver with fevered fright
Sick slick delusions
A witch! A witch torments!
"A black thing at the bed's feet"

*In Easthampton (then spelled as one word) in now modern New York in 1658, sixteen-year-old Elizabeth Gardiner Howell, delirious with a serious childbirth fever, accused Elizabeth "Goody" Garlick of bewitching her before she succumbed to the illness and died. Because of the intercession of the skeptical magistrate John Winthrop the Younger, Elizabeth Garlick was found not guilty and lived out the rest of her life.

Fresh Air

Move South, she mused

Where the air was clearer

Without a witchcraft conviction

She still had her life

And wished to live

Without a witchcraft conviction

*In 1670, after a witchcraft conviction in Wethersfield, Connecticut, Katherine Harrison hoped to start anew in Westchester County, New York, but her new neighbors had other ideas. When they tried to force her to move because of her reputation, the courts allowed her to live "where she pleased," and in 1672, she sued eleven of her neighbors for defamation of property.

Quote

Said William Penn in his colony
When he heard evidence against
Two women, Margaret and Gertro,
Accused of malfeasance,
If they had the legal right
To on a broomstick fly,
"I know no law against it."

*This famous quote came after the trial in Philadelphia, Pennsylvania, 1683, of Margaret Mattson and Gertro Jacobsson, who were accused of bewitching cattle and other animals, making threats, killing livestock, and appearing in spectral form. The Quaker William Penn conducted questioning himself, didn't allow attorneys, & permitted the introduction of unsubstantiated hearsay. Although they were found guilty of having the "reputation of a witch," they were not guilty of bewitching animals, and neither was convicted.

The One and Only

In the colony of Maryland

Long ago, long ago

A dozen were the trials

Or more so, or more so

But of all those accused

Here's the woe, here's the woe

Only one would feel the rope

Sadness grow, sadness grow

In the later land of Poe

It is so, it is so

*For Rebecca Fowler, the only person convicted and killed as a witch in the colony of Maryland, despite around a dozen witchcraft trials in the Province of Maryland in the 17th and 18th centuries. (She was executed on 9 October, 1685)

Wronged

One with the land

Without ownership

Not comprehending

Private property

Driven from hunting

Stopped gathering

Raised weapons defend

Protect family

Eyes dark as ravens

Hair smooth as shadow

Betrayed by white men

Scream battle cries

*During colonial times, the indigenous population was often viewed as devil worshippers and even devils themselves.
*While director of New Netherland from 1638 until 1647, William Kieft accused indigenous peoples of cursing him.

Apples and Accusations

Orchards bursting with temptation
Spirits in fine pewter cups
Red petticoats swish sarcasm
On villainy thou now sups

Outspoken and independent
Thrice married abused wife
Brass, Poppets, and tongue unbridled
Gone is thine trial of strife

*Bridget Bishop was the first person hanged as a witch during the Salem Witch Trials and the first woman hanged in the colony. She died on 10 June, 1692, proclaiming, "I am innocent."

Afflicted

Young women
And impressionable
Little girls
Who would otherwise
have scant or no
Agency
Launched into
Celebrity
Put on a deadly show

*The motivation of the afflicted remains a mystery to this day. Some scholars suggest they were impressionable young people influenced by adults with ambition for revenge or gain. Others point to a mass-hysteria or unknown ailment. Some even suppose the visions and feelings resulted from ergot poisoning, though this theory is largely dismissed. At the time in the 1690's, the people in Salem Village, Salem Town, and the outlying areas, lived in fear of attacks from hostile natives, of disease, of threatening weather, of starvation, of death, and yes, of the devil. Some of the afflicted repented and wrote apologies. All were children or young teens. Yet the question remains. What inspired the level of maliciousness that resulted in the imprisonment, ruinations, and death of so many neighbors?

Storyteller

Feed impressionable minds, my dear

With what they love and what they fear

A fortune told within an egg

Detect a spell with urine bread

Charm an Indian man and child

Repent, repent, and scream aloud

enslaved you have few human rights

You were given no means to fight

Confess to bigoted men, poor dear

Confirm suspicions, their greatest fear

*Inspired by Tituba, a person enslaved to the minister Paris and his family in Salem Village, 1692. Tituba was implicated for witchcraft, confessed, and under torture implicated two other women, Sarah Good and Sarah Osborne. She was never tried, but remained in prison until after the trial's 1693 conclusion. It's believed an unknown man paid her jail fees.

*Two other enslaved women were accused of witchcraft during the trials.

*Candy was enslaved to Margaret Hawkes of Salem Town. She confessed to using witchcraft but accused her mistress of signing the devil's book and turning her into a witch. She even retrieved poppets from their residence and demonstrated their use. Despite her confession and demonstration, she was found not guilty and released. No existing records indicate Margaret Hawkes was ever formally accused of witchcraft.

*Mary Black was the enslaved servant of Nathaniel Putnam. Relatives of Nathaniel Putnam accused Mary of witchcraft after he refused to back their complaint against a neighbor (Rebecca Nurse) and instead came out in support of her. Mary Black was not found guilty, her jail fees were paid by Nathaniel Putnam, and she returned to his service.

A Good Woman

Destitute and homeless
With young children to protect
Pregnant Sarah Good knocked
Begging neighbors for some food
To feed her hungry brood
Little Dorothy at her side
This marginal member of
The Salem community
With the reputation
Of outspoken ne'er-do-well
Became a perfect target
to be accused of witchcraft.
On 29 February, she, another Sarah,
And Tituba the servant
of the Samuel Parris home
Were arrested for afflicting
Little Betty Parris
and Abigail, her cousin.
Many others of her neighbors
Leveled accusations
Of Sarah's injurious actions
And spectral misbehaviour-
Even her daughter testified,
And her husband said she
Was not a witch "but close
to becoming one."
Sarah was the first tried

She never confessed, and
Only one man came to
Her defense, proving an accuser
Provided false evidence,
But Judge Stoughton dismissed
His sound defense.
Sarah was condemned, but
Her sentence would wait
Until she'd birthed her newest child.
While still held in prison,
That poor baby was born dead,
And Dorothy, her six-year-old
Confessed to being a witch
To be closer to her momma.
One hot morning in July
Sarah was taken
to the gallows where she said,
"I'm no more a witch than
you are a wizard!"
"If you take away my life,
God will give you blood to drink!"

*Written for feisty Sarah Good, victim of the Salem Witch hysteria

A Good Girl

So tiny, tricked testifying
Against her own momma,
So tiny, accused by Ann Putnam
Of spectrally choking and biting
So tiny, to try to trap Ann
By signing Satan's book
So tiny, maybe didn't know
How to read or write herself
So tiny, missing mother,
Interrogated for two weeks
So tiny, she broke down
And claimed a snake familiar
So tiny, crammed in prison
Clapped in irons, stood in filth
So tiny, watching women
Tortured, tear-filled, killed
So tiny, witnessed mother
Give birth to sister Mercy
Who, so tiny, never cried
And never breathed
So tiny, little Dorothy's
Momma pulled from prison
So tiny, to remain in jail
Knowing her mother died

*Dorothy (or erroneously recorded as Dorcas) Good, daughter of accused Sarah Good, was no more than six (and maybe as young as three) when she was herself accused by Ann Putnam of witchcraft. She was so small, they had to make special manacles and shackles for her. She was incarcerated in the Ipswich jail from 24 March until 10 December, 1692, when her father, William, finally raised the fifty pound bail and board to free her. By most accounts, she'd become insane and never recovered from the experience.

Brutal

Those accused were
Sleep-deprived, terrorized,
Humiliated, starved,
Abused and forced to sign
Admitting to falsehoods
Accused by young girls
With indefensible, absurd
"Spectral evidence"
Which was no evidence at all
Yet collaborated by a community
Of "pure" and "Christian" people
Accepted by men of learning
Damning those accused

*Written for Sarah Good, Sarah Wildes, Rebecca Nurse, Elizabeth Howe, and Susan Martin, who were all hung on my birthday (19 July) in 1692.

Family Affair

Three sisters grew in God's community and grace
Three sisters married, mothers, and productive
Three sisters innocent as the child unborn
Three sisters accused of witchcraft
Two sisters hung on Gallows Hill
Only one poor sister survived

*Rebecca Nurse, Sarah Cloyce, and Mary Eastey were all accused of witchcraft and tried. Seventy-one-year-old Rebecca, one of the oldest of the people accused during the Salem situation, and Mary Eastey met their end at the insistence of "The Afflicted."

Oft Maligned

Susanna, strong of mind and firm of faith
Conscience clear as a summer spring
Laughed at Afflicted folly in court
Finding such histrionics unbelievable
Accusing her accusers of themselves
Being under the influence of Satan
Quoting with authority God's word
(supposed to prove her innocence)
Still twenty-four people accused her
Of Satanic worship and collusion
While her past accusations cast suspicion
She clung to her Bible though she hung

*Susanna Martin was first accused of witchcraft in 1669. After a court case and suing for libel, she was cleared of charges only to face accusations again in 1692.

Disturbing

Pinch and prod,

Beat and brawl,

Hang until near dead

'Twas the Puritan's way

To prevent

A witch from casting spells

*Mary Webster of Hadley, Massachusetts became known as "half-hanged Mary" after a court acquitted her of witchcraft charges in 1683, but her dissatisfied neighbors wanted to prevent her from malfeasance. Their form of "disturbing" involved an unsuccessful lynching.

Salem

Peace
It's what you mean
Jerusalem relocated
Peace
Is not what you brought
To two hundred souls
Peace
Is what is wished
For the lives disrupted
For those wronged
For those who embrace
A conspicuous irony
Of Peace
In Salem

*These days, Salem, Massachusetts embraces its witchy reputation. The last of those convicted in the Salem Witch Trials were officially exonerated in 2022.

*According to court records, over two hundred people from Salem and surrounding areas were accused of witchcraft during the Salem Witch Trials of 1692-1693. Nineteen people, fourteen women and five men, were publicly hung as witches in Salem, Massachusetts during their trial. One man, Giles Corey, was publicly "pressed" to death when he failed to enter a plea. Even animals didn't escape the madness. Records show two dogs were also hung as witches' familiars. At least five other accused people died as a result of the deplorable conditions in the jails.

Evil Accusation

You are old, grandmother
And quite alone
With only your cats as friends
So you talk to yourself
Which isn't quite right
Further marks you apart
Gone are your good looks
Your husband is dead
No children nearby for comfort
No protections for self
Or for your choice lands
Only your wits and arthritic hands -
Such an easy accusation
Means property acquisition
With no one to argue your case

*The North American East Coast Colonies took their lead in legislative matters from England. Many factors, from fear of the unknown (and witchcraft in specific), hyper-religious ideology, unhappy native people and wars therewith, as well as environmental factors such as severe weather and its consequences and illness, could have contributed to the initial accusations. However, as with all such situations, in Salem, 1692-1693, specifically, opportunistic personalities seem to have manipulated the direction the accusations took.

"What have we learned? That in times of inhumanity, humanity is still possible. Even when there is hatred around...fight it. If I cannot fight the hatred all over the world, at least I can fight hatred somewhere, in one person, in me...for today, too, there are Salems." Elie Wiesel at the Salem Witch Trials Memorial Dedication, 1992

Curse bringer

On a frozen Febr'ry night,
Unfit for ev'n wild beasts
A mob of frightened, enraged souls
Pulled Moll from humble bed
They pointed blame and heaped hatred
Set fire to all she owned
Into the ice and blizzard dark
Moll ran 'til legs gave out
Collapsed upon a grave of stone
And with her final cry
Left hand to moon she called a curse
To punish vengeful souls

*Moll Dyer, was a resident of the outskirts of Leonardtown, Maryland, USA, St. Mary's County, who was accused of witchcraft and chased out of her home (which they burned) by townsfolk on a bitter winter night in 1697 or 1698 because they blamed her for bad harvests, unexpected deaths, harsh weather, and "the great epidemic." Her body was found days later, frozen to a stone, which is said to bear the indentations from her hand and knee prints. The 875 pound is today displayed as a tourist spot, but be warned. Legend says bad luck befalls all who venture too close.

*The area declared 26 February "Moll Dyer Day" in 2021, and a local road bears her name, too. Moll is also one of the inspirations for the film *The Blair Witch Project.*

There But by the Grace

Bound foot to arm behind aching back
Thrown into mucky water
Trusting the element would reject
One no longer baptized
And indicate a witch

Somehow she escaped this witchcraft test
Which proved her tainted as witch
In the colony of Virginia
Somehow she survived
Yet remained alive

*This is inspired by the "swimming ordeal" of Grace Sherwood in Virginia, 1706. She survived "swimming," which "proved she was a witch." She spent several years in prison before her 1714 release.

Skin

Satan left his mark
Upon her milky skin
A damning display

Prosecutors left their mark
Branded and lashed
into her milky skin

Executed and displayed
In a gibbet
Milky skin decomposing

Desiccated skin dug up
No longer milky
Morbid curiosity

*Maurice Josefte, somewhere around 1733 in Quebec was branded, lashed, and executed for murder, her body displayed in a gibbet. She was buried in the gibbet. It's said in 1851, her body was dug up and displayed.

Le Corriveau at the Crossroads

Marie married a farmer, had children, two daughters and a son,
That man died and left her a widow with three children
Then she married another man who died from a horse kick
In March, 1763, she and her father were tried for murder
Of the second husband by the newly-in-charge British
In Quebec City at the Ursulines of Quebec
In April, her father was sentenced to death, while Marie
Was to be lashed and branded with an M for murder but
Her father changed his story and accused his daughter
She confessed to killing him in his sleep using a hatchet
And was hung, her body displayed in an iron Gibbon
On the Buttes-a-Nepveu near the Plains of Abraham
At the crossroad of modern St. Joseph St. and de Lanta Blvd
She was buried in the gibbon

By the mid 1800's Marie's reputation had grown
The number of husbands and a reputation of maleficence
Swelled until in 1851 her grave was excavated
The gibbon in which her skeleton resided was purchased
And displayed by P.T. Barnum, given to the Boston Museum
And now is on permanent display at the Musée de la Civilisation in Quebec

*Marie-Josephte Corriveau still inspires novels, songs, and plays to this day

Inadmissible in Trial

New France in the seventeenth century
Did not allow
Supernatural or spectral evidence
To be admitted in a court case
Which means nothing
Impossible in nature
Like dreams or visions
Or witches marks
People could appeal death sentences
So courts preferred banishment
As a suitable punishment
For those deemed guilty

*Canada or "New France" had 22 court cases with witchcraft indicated. However, spectral & supernatural evidence was usually inadmissible in the trials.

Entangled Revenge

To prevent a witch from enacting
A fully justified revenge
Bury her upside down beneath a tree
Where the roots can entangle
And ensnare her intentions
Without marking her resting place
And disavow any knowledge of her fate
And then go about your lives
As if you didn't commit murder
And most likely theft as well
Praying the tree remains healthy
And doesn't release the enraged spirit
You've so terribly wronged

*The "Witch of Esperance" was a French widow in the late 1700's believed to practice maleficence, so the people in her town shot her while she made dinner and buried her upside down in an unmarked grave under a pine tree on the north side of the village.

Witching Power

A patriot doesn't need to be
A minute man or general
As the story of Hulda shows
And it is most memorable

Hulda spoke to apple trees
And lived in the woods alone
befriended the ghostly woman in white
Who at Raven Rock nightly moans

She danced with celestial maidens
Who waltzed from heavenly heights
and with her gun repelled a march
which fought off British mites

Not Dutch nor native, Hulda came
From European parts
She left herbal packets to heal
Ailing neighbors from her heart

Though not accepted in the Old Dutch Church
Hulda left a boon
Within her Bible, when she died
for widows were doubloons

*Hulda of Bohemia, Patriot, 1777 whose marker can be found in the Old Dutch Burial Grounds, outside the Old Dutch Church, Sleepy Hollow, NY, USA. Carla Lynn Hall performs a live retelling in "Hulda, the Other Legend of Sleepy Hollow" (Visit www.carlakeyes.com for more)

Inquisition Overloaded

The Holy Inquisition set up shop
In Mexico City to rid the place of witchcraft
The indigenous ancestors and spirits
Swirled with whoop and flame
The whisper-soft flutter of wings in the night
Of misfortune-bringing witch owls
That swoop to steal sweet babies
Herbal smokes blow over illness
Candles convey prayers, eggs contain spells
Traditions adapted and adopted
Challenged colonialism and
asserting ancestral strength

*On the proverbial eve of Mexican independence in the late 1700's, the Holy Inquisition in Mexico was so overwhelmed by the multitudes of cases of magical practices, witchcraft, and satanic pacts, it didn't even investigate most. The population was too spread out geographically and was too diverse and complex to effectively weed out the "magic problem."

*Magic is still practiced in Mexico today.

The Oppressors

The oppressors feared
A collective realization
by enslaved people
Who possessed tremendous strength
That they could overpower
The fearful oppressors

The oppressors used
Their society's witchcraft laws
Against those called slaves
To brutalize, cow, and kill
To control those left alive
After their latest oppression

*In 1741, fears of a slave revolt culminated in a frenzied witch hunt in Manhattan resulting in the deaths of 30 black enslaved people and 4 whites

Witch of Weare

Taker of the sweetest butter
Bitter hag whose name brought fright
Sickened any with a thought
Would on wintry, moonlit nights
Take to the cold, thin air
And cackle with delight

*Rhoda Dustin, whose husband ran an inn in Weare, was believed by the community to be a witch who could fly, inflict illness, and curse butter churns.

*Although she was never tried, she was a constant topic of gossip and recipient of "counter-curses," and she lived from 1736 until 1824, when she died of natural causes. She became a local Vermont legend.

Transformation

To see the dark devil
One needs a ride
So turn a friend
Into a steed

To display bold anger
One might make float
A neighbor's cow
Then drop to death

To punish injustice
Cast a mean spell
That causes foes
To vomit pins

To escape scrutiny
Transform into
Mountain lions
And black rabbits

*Four were tried, whipped, and had hot coals applied to their feet as punishment for practicing witchcraft in Winnsboro, South Carolina in 1792.

Rational Minds

What spell was cast by a young bride
To make her husband fall from a cliff
In an area he often trod?

How did so many serpents come to guard
The property of the widows weeds-wearer
Who never again married?

Why would an intelligent young woman
Not foretell an early widowhood would
Plunge her into poverty?

Who would be so brazen and bold
As to use her reputation as a witch
To extort food and firewood?

When a neighbor gave the smallest of
Her pies to the begging witch,
Why would she curse her?

Why would a fisherman who trespassed on
The widow's land to catch trout in her brook
Never catch another fish?

How, when two men in an oxcart
Stopped to mock the widow witch,
Did the wheels fall off?

Did Salem's trials haunt rationality
To allow a suspected witch to live
Largely unmolested to 76?

Did the death of a rooster named Old Boreas
Foretell the demise of the widow witch
Who made unfulfilled burial demands?

*Remembering Hannah Hovey (nicknamed Cranna) from Monroe, Connecticut (1783-1859) whose gravestone is located in Gregory's Four Corners Burial Ground.

Polly's Prophecy

Polly, dear Polly,
Heed my words
I've a warning for you
Do not go to
the White Rocks
With that man of yours.

Polly, dear Polly,
He means harm
To you his fiance
You're not his class
A serving girl
Not a match for that man of yours.

Polly, dear Polly,
You went though
Ignored warnings I gave
Up on the rocks
In white dress
To marry that man of yours.

Polly, dear Polly,

Why are you

Crushed at the hill's steep base

Among the rocks

Stained blood red

As the guilt of that man of yours.

Polly, dear Polly,

Your spirit

Cries among the white rocks

Wailing you're wronged

Unavenged

Killed by a man not yours.

*Based on an accurate prediction by Mary "Moll" Derry, a well-documented Witch from Western Pennsylvania, USA, in 1810. Polly Williams' fiancé, Philip Rogers, hired an expensive attorney and walked away without punishment for Polly's demise.

Queen Calling

Earth beneath long fingernails
Calloused feet unshod
Woman's waist wasted not
Wrapped in whitest white
Hair high and oil shiny
Eyes mysteries explored
Lips lush with languid learning
Smooth cinnamon skin bright
Rattling bones and dancing dolls
Summoned shadows skip
Ancestors and arachnids
Windy whispers whine
Smoke stilled inside impatience
Ecstatic magic mind

*Marie Laveau was a Louisiana Creole practitioner of voodoo, an herbalist, and a midwife whose renown continues to this day. Visitors still leave x's and offerings at the voodoo queen of New Orleans' tomb. Because she was also a hairstylist, many people leave offerings of bobby pins and hair ties. This devoted Roman Catholic also helped her community during outbreaks of illness. She died on 15 June, 1881 at nearly the age of eighty.

Disembodied Bell

Strange creatures walk the Tennessee land
Misshapen hares and harrowing hounds
They stare malice through foggy twilight

Knocks assault the house in Tennessee
Three sharp strikes upon the exterior
At all hours since the family moved in

Eerie whispers assail the children
A woman's voice emanating from walls
Biblical quotes and intelligent conversation

Invisible hands tore bedclothes from the beds
Ripped clumps of hair from the girls' heads
Slapped the youngest leaving angry red marks

General Andrew Jackson heard of the Bell Witch
Brought a witch-tamer to help the oppressed family
But the invisible, verbal witch pushed the tamer out

The witch hated John Bell, the father
Tormented him until his death
And continued to harass the family thereafter

*The Bell Witch (Tennessee, USA during the 1800's)
(Even Stonewall Jackson heard her)

Navajo Wisdom on Witchcraft

In Navajo traditional teachings,
A witch is one who is selfish
Denies what is good and right
It's about having power
And puts fear into the hearts and mind
Of other people to control them

If a coyote passes in front of you
Stop the journey. It gives you a warning.
Pray to Creator and think for yourself
And seek the guidance of Holy People
And you will have protection
To combat the Evil One

Body, Mind, Spirit, and Heart
All need protection from evil influence
Evil can be so well disguised that
It can appear as something good
Nobody likes to talk about evil
It gives power to a thing to talk about it

Tattoos and piercings can create openings
For evil to sneak in and enter a body
Always be aware of cheats and misinformation
These things can lead to corruption
Evil destroys families and unity

Demons are not physical but influence
And help evil which opposes good
Witchcraft is one of the ways demons
Can influence the five-fingered world
Using the witch as a physical agent
They distract people from what's right and good

*From the wisdom found at
www.navajotraditionalteachings.com
*Navajo People have magic of their own, but they don't call it witchcraft. To them, witchcraft is a selfish, controlling, evil act influenced by demons.

Roadside Grave Magic

In Kirtland Hills in Northeastern Ohio
At the Crossroads of Hart and Baldwin
At the far edge of an 1814 family farm
Is the "Witches' Grave"
This family's gravesite
Of Levi and Ruth Smith is
Surrounded by a partial stone wall
With a slab and oval and broken bit
Of cemetery stone atop and
As visitors walk away to leave
If they look over their shoulder
They will notice the stone moved
Proving the family's witchcraft
Is still supernaturally strong

*The original gravestone for the Smiths was moved because of its historical significance in the area. The Smiths helped establish the community in the early 1800's after setting up their homestead after moving from Derby, Connecticut. The existing stones are the 1988 replacements.

Winter of Long Shadows

Calls from Raven's Hollow
Along by Witches Bend
Family secrets strangle
From the twisted trees
Children hear the sirens
Luring from the dirt
Teaching arcane substance
With languages unknown
To the mountain people
A supernatural storm
Bringing death and waking souls
Long moldered in the ground
Babies born not human
Vessels of the unknown
Singing haunting choruses
Shared by enlightened minds
Traveling the Devil's Backbone
Within the Cumberland Gap

*A spate of witchcraft accusations rocked the mountain folk in Appalachia, USA between 1878 and 1889.

Connect Latinx

Connect past and present

Manifest an abundant future

Wrongs righted

Fortune smiled

Upon spiritual forerunners

Of ancestral acclaim

*Brujería refers to magical practices in Latin America. It adopts Mexican cultural elements with spiritual traditions and Catholicism.

Santeria

Interacting with Orishas
A white Dove flying free
Candles and meditations
Sixteen blessed Cowrie
Coconut, palm, and ceiba
Knives and Elekes
Dancing together
Blended blessed be

*Santeria blends Afro-Cuban religion with Yoruba traditions and Catholicism.

Macumba

Candomble and Umbanda
African religions
Brujos invoke Orixas
Spirits in the nature
Catholic traditions
Seeking what's hidden
Native wisdom
Spiritual seeking
Be it light or Cuca
Cultures combined
A magical concoction
Brilliant Brazilian blend

*Witchery in Brazil, actually in all of South America, combines many cultural, religious, and spiritual beliefs.

Yara

High on Sorta Mountain
Near the town of Chivacoa
A goddess with eclipse hair
Accepts alms from her faithful
Her mount a golden tapir
Dances to spiritual drums
She oversees the other seeing
Of those who worship her
Allows ancestral visits
In the shadows of her home

*Yara is the indigenous alternative name of Maria Lionza of Venezuela

Afar

Witching Far and Wide

Ancient practices were made evident
Within the famed Code of Hammurabi
Babylonian witchcraft is present
In historical tracts like the Torah
And Quran and condemned as evil acts
In India, "Dayan" is not allowed
An adopted colonial belief
And is persecuted even today
Two thousand people in twelve years*
Chinese witchcraft is deeply mystical
With traditional practices, and yet
Gong Tau in China and the Southeast
Enacts black magic against another
Dukun are Malaysian and Sumatran
Magicians who cause illness and misfortune
Colonizers in the Philippines, too,
Subjugated shamanic spell casting
'Til now witches use only the dark arts
Or so certain folks would have us believe
Vietnamese witchcraft connects with gods
So "ba dong" can perform magical acts
Korean "Musok" is on the upturn
Despite some residual stereotypes
Shinto in Japan is shamanistic
some convey positive connotations
Though foxes can make tricky familiars
Reclaimed folk beliefs are being embraced
By many of Asia's younger people
Meanwhile Wicca gains a following, too

The Fields Remained Barren

The fields remained barren
Where the witches were killed
On the Barbados island
Where twilight bears voices
Of dark eyed women
Enslaved and wronged
Crying for justice
In an unjust world
Where a planter's daughter's dreams
Determine their final fates
Until the fields remained barren
Where the women were killed

*1650 Barbados

Obeah

On the islands in the Caribbean
Surrounded by azure waters
That lap sun-soft sands
Winds blow salty breezes
As a crucible of cultures
Blends heritage and faith
To promote the power of endurance

*Obeah is one word for Caribbean witchcraft designed by many enslaved people and their descendants. It's a personal, adaptable belief system blending African, Indigenous, and Western Christian religions. It was demonized and eventually criminalized to try to control possible slave uprisings (like Tacky's Rebellion).

Scientist

Not where she's meant to be
Betrayed, enslaved
dehumanized
Indomitable will still
West African practices
Framed understanding
Retained spiritual ancestry
European folk practices
Christian and Indigenous
Island beliefs
Heal and harm
Protect and curse
Claimed cultural currency

Dayans

In swirling Sanskrit
References to Dayans
(or Witches) emerge
With wide, dark eyes
And darker intentions
Innocence wrapping rot

*The Santhal Witch Trials of 1792 are some of the earliest recorded Witch Trials in India. It's believed there were others, but scholars suspect these were mob-instigated and executed cases, quick, brutal, unrecorded, and outside the standard auspices of the law.

*During the colonial era in India during the 19th century, with records indicating over a thousand women were killed on the grounds of witchcraft in the Central plains region alone.

*Male magic practitioners called Bohpas or Bahgats were employed to identify female witches. They then used their 'powers' to 'exorcise' the magic out of the women. Some aspects of their powers included torture and execution.

Curandera

Born in bondage
Enslaved and sexualized
She earned freedom
Plied a trade in charms
Healer or curandera
Rewarded and respected
Stunning beauty and beguiling
Dressed fashionably
Object of male attention
And of jealous rumors
Accused of witchcraft
Not once but thrice
Deported to Cartagena de Indias
From her Island home
Called on connections
Who owed their lives
To her magic ministrations
Provided testimonies
She endured humiliations
Maintained her innocence
Beat all of the charges
With her wit and friendships

*Paula de Eguiluz faced the Inquisition in 1624, when she confessed and was sentenced to 200 lashes administered in public and a stay in a penitent's hospital. Again, charges were leveled against her in 1632, but she gave the names of 21 other suspected witches, assured that her herbal remedies were only meant for good, and called on some influential contacts to vouch for her. Her final trial was in 1634 when some of the women she accused testified against her. Records indicate she was found guilty and sentenced to death, but a bishop she aided interceded.

Mystic Island

In tropical mountains
Hidden in the hills
Witches heal and help
Expel evil entities
Deflect hexes and curses
Herbs and mists, faith, and fears

*The Philippine Island, Siquijor, is known for its benevolent Witches that blend shamanistic traditions with Catholicism.

Ancestors and Ancients

African mysticism
Informs many beliefs
Spirits of all things
Components of the craft
Exert influence over
The spiritual realm
Overtaken with ancestors
Practicing protection
Misguiding misfortune
Dark and light together
Directed with intent

*African magic has been incorporated into many other belief systems around the world, sometimes couched into Christianity by enslaved African people as a way to assert some agency in an otherwise powerless existence.

Insights

To Fly

It was said in court reports
Witches to Sabbath fly
To do so they concocted
An ointment dark and dire
thus:
Anoint a broomstick or other phallus with
The juice of smallage, snake foil, and wolfsbane,
fine wheat and
the rendered fat of newborn babe
Or so the recipe suggests
With variations that include Nightshade,
Mandrake, Henbane, and Jimsonweed
This psychedelic concoction was applied
to the broomstick and ridden, sometimes naked,
Exposing the ointment to personal parts
Or the ointment was applied directly to underarms
Which feeds the elements into the thirsty
bloodstream

*The first known illustrations of witches on brooms is from Martin Le Fanc's Le Champion des Dames, 1451

Familiar Spirits

Come to the heartsong
Invisible ones
Come dear companion
Befriend the lonely
Come as a black cat
Or other animal
Come and bring ease
No matter your form
Come and be fed
With the milk of kindness
Come share in the work
Of soft, humble hands
Just come, oh, please come
Succor and friendship
Come, fair familiar
And meet your new witch

*Familiar Spirits are known as interdimensional beings, supernatural entities, spirit guides, and helpers who assisted witches in their magical work. Traditional familiars came in fairy, human, or animal form, corporeal or as spirits. Some animal spirits included in court reports include the cat, toad, dog, bird, hare, ferret, rat, goat, sheep, horse, frog, butterfly, fly, wasp, and pig. But they come in all shapes and sizes. Black hides nicely in shadows, so animals with black fur or skin, particularly those that traverse at night, were viewed with particular caution. The black cat continues to be considered a symbol of bad luck to this day.

For example from the Pendle Witch Trial:
Ball-Elizabeth Device's familiar spirit, a brown dog
Dandy-James Device's familiar spirit, often a brown dog
Fancy-familiar spirit of Anne Chattox
Tibb or Tibbs-familiar spirit of Elizabeth Demdike

From a woodcut in Matthew Hopkins' Discovery of Witches book, Familiars were named:
Vinegar Tom, Pecke in the Crowne, Griezzdl Greedigutt, Sacke and Sugar, Newes

Some others named in various sources:
Tom Reid-invisible familiar of Besse Dunlop of Scotland
Queen of Elphame-fairy queen that aided Isobel Gowdie
Tyffin (white lamb), Tittey (gray cat), Pigeon (black toad), Jack (black cat) helped Ursula Kemp, according to her 8-year-old son, Thomas Rabbet. Ursula confirmed this under torture.
Three spirits: one like a cat, called Lightfoot, another like a toad, called Lunch, the third like a weasel, called Makeshift.

Familiars are sometimes simply called Devil, imp, familiar, fairy, elf, or goblin.

Afflicted Visions

Pricked with pins and tied in knots
Sung to by a yellow bird
Set upon by vicious dogs
That none but the girls could see
Twisted, tortured, and tormented
Assailed by spectral visions dark
Of people from the village
Intent upon harming all
Who refused to sign their name
Sickened, soured, and forsaken
Cats crawling across the roof
Books of red and books of black
A shadowed man in a heavy hat
Called from deep within the woods
Where savagery bedevils
The goodly minded maid

*The Afflicted in Salem during the 1692-1693 trials complained of all of these things.

Hag Ridden

It was once believed
Witches wandered at night
Rode animals or men
Spectral excursions

Animals kidnapped
Lathered from their run
Weakened, injured, ill
cross in the morning

Some owners abused
Abandoned or mistreated
Hag-ridden beasties
Though they were blameless

People thus misused
Were stolen from dreams
Woke exhausted and sick
Listless and angry

Bestest Bois

Two dogs died
Victims of
The Salem panic

One was shot
For bewitching
An afflicted girl

This dog was
Innocent
Said Cotton Mather

None could kill
The Devil
Even in disguise

The dog died
Which meant he
Was not bewitching

Another dog
Thought hag rode
In Salem Village

Behaved odd
The people
Hung the dog victim

*Two dogs were recorded as killed during the Salem witch hysteria.

Key

There is a key to magic
Which is to use a widow's key
Placed in a bowl of cold water
Pour melted lead over it
To form prophetic shapes
Which is particularly powerful
At Samhain and liminal times-
Or align an antique key
By sleeping with it under a pillow
Or use moon magic to cleanse
Or in the salty sea
Or other running water-
A key can guide a questor
To a new home by suspending
It from a hair or string
To dowse over a map-
Inscribe the key with
Sigils, signs, or words
And wear it to help guide
To a brand new home-
Keys can serve as talismans
To protect and heal a home-
Place a key along the spine
To stop a nose from bleeding
There is a magic in a key

Plant Protections

Rowan, mighty mountain ash,
Whose branches embrace
And berries protect
Hazel wands want Mayday charges
Vervain, yarrow, and Foxglove
Mix in black cat hair, Primrose in bloom
Daisy chains on heads, Thumbs in milk
Painted on animals for protection
Red ribbons, Brigit's crosses
Four-leafed legacy in emerald land

Cailleach

Connected to
A living culture
Embedded in green
Burrowing through
Burial mounds
into standing stones
Dancing on fluted
Fairy rings and forts
Dug deep in antiquity
Culturally rooted

*Cailleach is a Gaelic word for witch.

Disguised

A hunter in the Highland lands
Came upon a hare,
Took aim and fired but soon found
The creature unaffected
It raised its lip in a sneer
And asked in croaky voice,
"Unmannered boy, would you, would you
So treat your mother?"

*It was presumed witches could assume the form of animals.

Witch's Wells

Make a wish
within the heart
Drop a coin -
An offering
To the well's spirit
The wish comes true

Brew

Sisters, gather round midsummer's fire
Fear not its flames, no funeral pyre
Within our cauldron we shall brew
Elegant potions, an immortal stew
With queer-sounding herbs and newborn fat
With our familiar, a mighty black cat

Tiny Sacrifices

To hold a little bundle
wrapped in homey rags
Hear the coo and see the firsts -
Smiles, words, rolls -
Sacrificed for favor
Of Satan and his spawn

Sabbat

Called with intent, they gather
Within forbidden, dark woods
A bonfire crackles chaos
They cast aside their dark hoods

They fly on phallus unfettered
Kiss their dark master's behind
Exchange songs and incantations
Transformed in heart and in mind

Dance with lustful abandon
Ingredients with fanciful names
Sign the black book of magic
The Devil each lost soul reclaims

*It was believed witches would gather at Sabbats (Sometimes called Black Masses or Black Sabbaths - had to give Ozzy's band a shout out!) under cover of darkness in far-flung places like deep woods to perform rituals, worship the devil, initiate new witches, and other such things.

Dance for the Devil

Little children tell of magic-filled nights
When they "Ride" sleeping men to an island
These men stay in a multi-colored barn
While the children join multitudes of witches
They feast on meats, rich butter, and such sweets
They've never before or since encountered
They drink dark red wines like those in a church
Til their heads and bodies won't stop spinning
Some women sit on their heads, bums up, naked
with black candles aflame in their bumholes
The children join a parade of witches
To dance for the devil's dark pleasure

*This is taken from an account concerning a Blokulla, or the Swedish idea of a hidden island or meadow where the devil held court during witches' sabbaths.

Lest the Dark Words Take Hold

Envy crushes spirits
Invokes the Evil Eye
Ward against it by spitting thrice
Over the left shoulder
Banish bad energy

Whispers of destruction
Crops withered, cattle ill
True curses spoken with intent
Summon uneasy spirits
To torment for generations

Words over knots and pins
Incantations ancestral
The old ways enacted
Or evolved to improve
effective spell crafted effects

Wards

Salt sprinkled in liminal spaces
A line of powdered brick dust, too
Holy Water to bless and purify
Sage smoke smudges clear negativity
Glass balls to disorient and capture
Strange bits of architecture included
To discourage unwanted visitors
Geometry made magic talismans
Apotropaic witchmarks carved deter
Natural protections from plants brought home
Thorns, pinecones, tree sap, and certain stones
Holed hagstones for true sight and protection
Prayer protects and provides a barrier
Many Blessings and rituals keep safe

Hallowmas Raid, The Witches' Ride
or,
Methods of flight for witches

Crush well your Eggshells,
Else they may be
Made into witch's boats.
Lock up brooms, though
Ragwort, or other stalks
Can be made by witches to fly
Secure your livestock,
say your prayers,
And hang an iron horseshoe
For witches can upon these ride
To their Hallowmasses
As well as on hares, cats, chickens.
High Ranking witches, though,
Are conveyed in chariots
Made from a dead man's bones,
The seat sewn from the skin
of newborn children,
While from Satan's own forge
Came the metal bits binding it all together.

*These historical descriptions are reminiscent of tales of the Wild Hunt

Pricker

Needles and pins and other devices
Pressed into tender flesh
The accused shaved bald
And stripped entirely bare
Often before the community
In a time of extreme modesty
And all parts explored
With needles and pins
And other sharp devices
Pressed into tender flesh
By a witch pricker
In search of a witch spot,
An insensitivity,
Without bloody discharge
A mole, a callous, a blemish, a scar
Used to suckle a familiar
Or mark the touch of Satan

Little Prick

Looking for a witch spot
An illusive little thing
Insensitive and unbleeding
Proved relations with the devil

*Christian Caddell disguised herself as a man, renamed herself John Dickson, and, armed with a thick metal poker, hired out her services as a witch pricker. She made 6 shillings a day plus another 6 pounds for every identified witch, good money when the average salary was a shilling a day.
*She pricked a member of the royal court who successfully petitioned for her removal. She was discovered as a woman and banished to the colony of Barbados.
*The day she was transported to Barbados, 4 May, 1663, was also the day some of her victims were burned in Forres.
*Her findings led to the death of at least six people.

Swimming

Innocence or guilt
The water tells the tale
Those without a soul
Float in a water well

Water rejects anyone
Who rejects baptism
Innocent would drown
Which causes a schism

This uncanonical test
Without Biblical backing
Was not done often
Fees sent testers packing

*Swim Tests, with dunking chairs or when a person was trussed and tied and thrown into water, would indicate a witch if the person survived. An innocent drowned or was pulled out before their death. Either way, the poor soul could perish as a result of the test.

Silence, Witch

There Will Be No Incantations
Nor Seduction From Your Tongue
Fitted Out With Sharp Metal
You Reap What You've Begun

You'll Call No Foul Familiars
To Aid You In Your Plight
The Bridle Brings But Silence
And Ends Your Devilish Fright.

*Scold's Bridle/witch's bridle/gossip's bridle/brank's was a cruel, iron instrument with 4 sharp prongs forced into the accused's mouth, so that 2 prongs pinched and secured the tongue, and 2 pressed against the cheeks which was used to torture suspected witches, gossips, and scolds. Not only did it cause pain, but it also provided public humiliation.

Waking the Witch

Days of waking
In cells too small
To rest wearied bodies
Doused with water
And left to shiver
Shaken violent awake
Made to walk near collapse
Beaten, berated, starved
Until body failing,
Mind hallucinating,
The accused confessed
Of fanciful things
That exonerated their captor's
Evil actions

*Sleep deprivation was an accepted torture to extract confessions from those accused of witchcraft. Modern medical evidence explains the cumulative effects of sleep deprivation go beyond the loss of specific functions, because it ultimately causes a fatal decline of all functions, resulting in an inability to heal or mentally process. Hallucinations and physical pain accompany sleep deprivation.

Tipping the Scales

Lighter than Holy Bibles
Wispier than air
Rejected by God's waters
Soulless witches fare
Poorly during weigh-ins
When the two compare

*Oudewater had a weighing house and scale used to detect if a person accused of witchcraft retained their soul. The idea was a witch surrendered his soul and therefore weighed less than an honest person. The people who operated the scale would issue a certificate to prove the weighed innocence.
*The Museum De Heksenwaag displays the livestock scale used to determine innocence and guilt.
*Monty Python had a skit in their Holy Grail where an accused witch is weighed against a duck.

Torturous

The means varied
Depending on locale
But extraction of confession
Was the aim-
Be it with the strappado,
Arms tied behind,
Hoisted into the air,
Shoulders pulled from sockets,
Weights sometimes added
To increase the pain-
Or with the Spanish boot
Which crushed the bones
Of feet and legs
Like thumbscrews and other vises-
Flogging, binding, stretching, screams,
The human mind with torture teems!
Removal of body parts, racks, and wheels,
Torture's false confessions revealed Ooooo!

*Implements of information extraction varied depending on the region, religion, and time period. Torture doesn’t produce true confessions.

Why?

If witches were so powerful
Grown men quaked before their might
Why didn't they free themselves
And give those folks a real fright?

Why accuse a wealthy widow
Condemn her to Hellfire
Except the upshot of the charge
Her goods you can acquire

So many accused "witches"
Had no one to defend them
Outcasts loners malcontents
Didn't fit their system

Words

Wise Women
Wyrd Women
Wily, Witty, Wonderful

Wild Women
Willful Women
Working, Witchy, Whimsical

Witches Wild and Free

Diaphanous Daughters
Unbowing and proud
Hair knotted with
starfire secrets
Tangled with turmoil
Twisted, turned
Elfin enchanters
Sweet spellbound songs
Lusty and lusted after
Unapologetic
Opinionated
Outspoken outsiders
Unbridled tongues
Hissing acidic curses
Into patriarchal soil
While willing wonders
With womanly wiles

Intuition

Subtle cues interpreted
Signs in everyday
Quiet, inner voices
Heeded

Warnings warring With reason
Urgent feelings filled
Stomach sending symbols
Listened

Otherworldly Wisdom owned
Synchronicity
Coincidental calms
Noted
understood

Witches' Marks

Protection of residences
carved in corners
Etched into edges
Hidden in overhangs
Painted power
X's and crosses
Spirals circling still
Stars and double vv's
Solomon's seals
Charmed and countercursed
Complex coded cyphers
Stopping evil intentions
Before entering a home

*Witch Marks are sometimes found in historical houses, churches, and public buildings, often at entries, hearths, windows, and the like to prevent evil from entering a dwelling. Some were placed on furniture and household items as well.

Inhuman

Descended of Nephilim
Or of the line of Cain
Huge appetites for all delights
Magic ways ingrained

Embodiment of winter
Cold strength and deadly grace
Biting Bertha, present Perchta
Danced a different pace

Disguised as human woman
No daughter yet of Eve
Of Lilith's line and Jinn defined
Narnia deceived

Great goddesses diminished
Stripped of divinity
Ability mere vanity
Forced fragility

*Some ancient scholars believed witches were not really entirely human. Some imagined them the descendants of Nephilim (giants born when fallen angels mated with human women). In the frozen Alpen areas, the personification of winter became associated with (or became) witches, and goddesses like the Greek Hekate and the Irish Brigit were rewritten as witches, demons, or saints, depending on the interpretation. In C.S. Lewis' children's stories, Jadis the White Witch seems to represent all of these, from her association with winter to her inhuman heritage.

NicNevin

Daughter Divine
Witch goddess mine
Emerge from murky past
Finish incomplete tasks
Drawing down magic fine

Songsteress

Hippy happy moonbeam mad
Twisting with mood music
Sleeves souring wrists wound
Around the songster's spell
She embodies angel sinners
Worming into collective cults

Gris Gris

Finger looped fragments
Of homespun delight
Caught intentions knotted
Into herbal remedies
Unbroken bones strengthened
Woven jewelry round the neck

Spellwork

Silver platter saving pins
Performed songs perfection sought
Sacrificed blood sacred bright
Begged symbols by soulfire

Piscadera

She comes in the night
To sit on the chest
Of innocent sleepers

The sleeper can't move
Can't scream, barely breath
As she laughs and stares

Her crushing weight
Squeezes like panic
As she sups on the fear

*Piscadera is the South American word for Night Hags. Night Hags are a phenomenon felt all over the world. Psychologists believe these are interpretations of Sleep Paralysis. Apparently at least 5 percent of the population will experience this terrifying condition at least once in their life.

Cachiche

A refuge for women
Accused of witchcraft
Fleeing the Inquisition
A town in Ica
Where Peruvians found
Comfort and protection

*Julia Hernandez Pecho, a renowned healer and witch, is associated with this one-time refuge.

On Hearts and Minds

To capture a heart
A skittish fickle thing
Takes confidence confined
By a magical mind
Will unwavering

Nightcrossed

Singing with starlight
Moonbeam pinned hair
Eyes wide as curiosity
Reaching for eternity
With crystal coated nails

Midlife Magic

Silver streaks like comets
Through summer soft tresses
Wink witty wisdom while
Evidence of experience
Smudges humility written
In hollows of dark-eyed wonder
And spider-fine spell work sung
To the soulful setting sun

Sleep slips into memory
Still dreams steal center stage
No longer pushed to prop up
Ambitions of the others
Who won without witchery
A harried, humbled heart
And without salves or broomsticks
Scattered sailing far from home

Perfect Start

Wash with dew at dawn
Bathe in morning mist
Place pansies in pots
Twist rosemary rings
Into hair braid beads
Gild garlands and wreaths
Stir coffee clockwise
Sprinkle cinnamon
With blessings and prayer
Let the day begin

Dumb Summer

Need to know who you'll marry?
Keep quiet and bake a cake
Using salt and flour
Not a sound nor ev'n a squeak
After it's done baking
Place atop it an iron knife
At midnight your mate will enter
And cut the cake with it
But beware!
If he makes even a whisper,
You must use that iron knife
To kill him

*This is an Irish legend that was carried to the Appalachian area.

Prognosticate Future Mate

Peel an apple in one piece
And toss the peel ov'r a shoulder
It will form the initial of
The thrower's fated lover

Or create a Venus glass
By pouring water in a bowl
Crack an egg and see the shape
Interpret the symbols

Robert Burns uses three dishes
Filled with water, foul and fair,
And one left empty to not marry
To learn spousal status with care

In Austra-Germany they set
A table for two without forks
Which calls the lover's spirit
Who will leave something behind

Holidays are special times
To tell who next will wed
St. Andrew's Eve or Christmas
Halloween or Midsummer

You Are

You know the woods and know the fauna
You're friends with the little folk
You know your heart and that of others
Actions when your intentions spoke

You feel the voices and feel emotion
Your own you harbor in the bones
You see the wonder in creation
You love even the largest tomes

You're drawn to crystals drawn to nature
The future plays out before your eyes
You're in touch with elementals
Ever filled with wonder and surprise

Visions

Flowers float, a phantom folly
Waves of water wander by
Flames flicker a fancy focus
A toss of bones on which to scry

Mirror magic, crystal gazing
Lay a tarot's painted spread
Doze while spinning, mind to wander
Drink a tea until the dregs

Hieromancy looks to entrails
Study spots where birds do nest
Pendulum swings and church bells ringing
Notice changes and unrest

Apple peels and stems foretelling
Open books to learn the truths
Foods prepared and how they're rotting
Melting wax, suspicious proofs

Mists and steam and cloudforms passing
Beads and bobs and tiny things
Infant response and pets proclaiming
Who first to the mailman brings

Words overheard or something missing
Pennies dropped and coins claimed
Pins and needles, threads for sewing
On this and more are visions blamed

Dolly

Made of grains or shaped of clay
Bits of cloth and stolen hair
Carved of fruit or knotted string
Crafted with purposeful care
These effigies represent
witch's enemies' despair

*In folklore and witchcraft, poppets are created to represent a person to aid or harm them. Finding such items could be used as evidence at witchcraft trials. Poppets have been found within the walls and chimneys of many old buildings across the globe. Of course, children have long cherished dollies as playthings, as well, and might not have been used for any other magic than that of a child's imagination.

Dolls for the Deceased

A little representative
Left to hold a space
Indicating gratitude
Perhaps
For the extraction of pieces
Of human remains
Used for necromantic ends

*Binding Dolls have been found in ancient Greek and Roman grave sites, where body parts were extracted from the corpse. It is believed these parts were used by a witch, with the doll left behind either as a sort of acknowledgement or payment or to bind the deceased to the magical act or the witch who performed it.

Kitchen Witch

Bid the bread to rise
The butter remain sweet
Keep infestation from this house
No burns to any meat

*This type of doll is still used today, often depicted as an old woman on a broom and hung in kitchens, sometimes stuffed with herbs, small crystals, and a charm.

The Left Hand Path

An heretical calling
Lures power motivated
Ringing revenge
Black blessings, too
Swim against the stream
Through darkness
Into occult corners
Many others avoid
To friend fearsome foes

From Within and Beyond

Cast the bones, throw marked stones
Interpret their patterns
Hear the message from the cards
See signs among the stars
And shapes left in left tea leaves
Scry in shiny gazing balls
Stare into a mirror
Observe the way of wild things
Messages from the unseen
Sent through pendulum swings
Dousing wires, sacred fires
Tell the future, see the past
Sent guidance from beyond
Wisdom from within

*The means of prognostication and fortune telling are as varied as the tellers themselves.

Hedgewitchery

Intuitive and personal
With magic woven in
To everyday activities
Savvy hedgewitch strides
In balance with the
Boundaries between
The villages and
The wildernesses
And the many realms
Of spirits and the wee ones
With herbs and folk beliefs
Never caught in
crystalline configurations
But wild wind free
With Spirit guides
and guards
Thus hedge witches be

Auntie April

She washed with April dew
To maintain her youthful beauty
Scattered ashes from the hearth
Onto her flower beds
To bless and enrich the blooms
Whose perfume persuaded
Peace from all who visited
And visit oft they did
She sung with the spring frogs
To bring the healing showers
And made gifts of tinkling iron
To hang in newborns' rooms
She flirted with both snowflakes
And the promised blazing sun
And bid welcome to
professed longer days
With Morning Mimosas and
Bewitching Weep No Mores.

Witchling

There's magic in the air tonight
Breathe deep of its powers
Where mystics make memories
Ambitions to devour
And all the lovely soulsongs
Repose in ancestral bowers
So breathe deep little witchling
Upon you blessings shower

Bedecked

Sprinkle salt like heartfelt wishes
Ingest moonbeams with your dreams
Don yourself with silvered dishes
Fragrant off'rings in blood streams

May Queen

A tussle in your hedgerow, so you know
A maiden dressed in white and floral crowned
She could be Mother Mary, Purity
Yet somehow she's fertility abloom
Flower-filled, enigmatic entity
A queen of fairies with her sylvan court
Pagan goddess of fragrant offerings
A call for help, repeated, repeated
Processed before Edwardian parades
In Midsommer, danced to near exhaustion
Last woman standing around the Maypole
Pay tribute to her on the first of May
With baskets of blooms left for your neighbors

*According to legend and popularized by song, The Black One induced the young of Hurga in Sweden to dance until they died at Midsummer. *This is depicted in the Ari Aster film, Midsommer, 2019

Bonfires

Bonfires burn, darkening the sky
To confuse witches passing by
On the brooms on which they fly
Communities protected thereby

*In some areas, particularly in Europe, bonfires are lit on nights like Walpurgis Night (30 April) or Beltane, Sankt Hans Aften. In Finland, Denmark, and Norway, the tradition with bonfires is observed on St. John's Eve (23 June) to confuse witches flying to their Sabbaths or as a fertility rite. Additionally, Easter is a popular bonfire date in some areas.
*Bonfires also were supposed to protect children and livestock. Some places have the children of the community dress as rosy-faced witches and sing for treats. (In a bit of irony, some people collect the ash from the bonfires because they are believed to have special powers to raise crops, and people would walk their cattle through the ashes to ensure fertility.)

Wiccan Wheel of the Year

Eight Sabbats to embrace
Holidays to celebrate
Divide the year like a pie
Solar and earth with moon mentions

Quiet introspection
The crone becomes a mother
Winter's settled comfortably
Yule, the shortest day of the year

Groundhogs nibble grasses
A maiden opens her eyes
Behold awakened splendor
Imbolc, when spring stirs up life

Bunnies bounce, renewal
Light and dark, exact balance
Harmonious symphony
Ostara, sweet Spring Equinox

Maiden moves toward mother
Randy spores and sperm spill wide
Beltane fertility rules
Masculine and feminine mixed

Longest day, shortest night
Crops reach full maturity
A time for personal growth
Litha, brightest Midsummer day

Cross quarter holiday

Lammas, harvest season starts
Goddess leads her children home
Full of abundant gratitude

Another day of balance
The goddess ready for rest
No darkness lasts forever
Mabon, autumnal equinox

Halloween, autumn queen
Holiday with many names
The Witches' New Year begins
On Samhain, veils between realms thins

*These celebrate the changes of the seasons. This division was formalized by contemporary Wiccan practitioners, with the Northern hemisphere in mind.
*dates: Yule (19-21 December), Imbolc (1 February), Ostara (19-21 March), Beltane (30 April-1 May), Litha (20-22 June), Lammas (1-2 August), Mabon (21-24 September), Samhain (31 October-1 November)
*Many of these holidays have other names depending on the area and belief system. Many even have Christian holidays, too, including Candlemas, Annunciation, May Day, Midsummer, St. John's Day, Lammas, All Hallows Eve/All Saints Day, and Christmas

Seasons

Flowers bloom, fauna thrives
Spring Equinox returns life

Bright bounty, beachy vibes
The Summer Solstice shines

Leaves changing, pumpkins glow
Autumn Equinox veils thin

Sparkling white, shining bright
The Winter Solstice shimmers

Heavens Knows

The moving of the cosmos
Twisting discernible paths
Gives hints into the future
To chart the person's birthplace
In the twinkling of the stars
And the streak of a comet
Come portents plenty foretold
As by ancient wise people
astronomical events
astrological success
by the moon are rites performed
Its tidal tribute taken
Solar solemnity seen

June

Gold glows bright, a brilliant beacon of becoming
Tempered by a strawberry moon
Accelerated growth flowering and flowing
Fruitful explosions of flavor
Beloved boys' birth, perfect bridal blush
Sunflowers, seashells, and fine sand

Soupy Spellcraft

Spidery script
An ancient book
Ancestral ingredients
Properly prepared
Breathed between
Lives and ages
Tastes and times
Culinary curiosity
Shared spellwork

NicNevin

Daughter Divine
Witch goddess mine
Emerge from murky past
Finish incomplete tasks
Drawing down magic fine

Accidental Witchcraft

Into an iron cauldron
Placed o'er a burning brand
She sprinkled ingredients.

Web of a wolf spider
Gathered at the dawn,
Ten crumbled Christmas cones...

Intuitive spell craft
She practiced, but a child,
As she stirred the bubbling brew.

Fungus from the fairy ring
found beneath the oak
Dried and powdered to dust...

Seen only by the wild things
Deep in her family's woods
Sheltered by tall timbers

Lucky four leafed clover,
Dandelion fluff,
A shedded serpent skin...

Her sweat and tears tumbled
Into the iron pot
Making wishes come true.

*First published in Poetic Nightmares by the author, 2023.

How Women are Perceived

An important lesson to remember
What is said says more about
The speaker than the subject
So some say a woman with power
is demeaned
By calling her a witch
Historically witches were
Emasculating monsters
Preserving penises on trees
Subverters of femininity
Trailblazers of the terrible
Embodiments of every
Miserable, misogynistic nightmare

Threshold

Danger on the doorstep
Liminal spaces saved
Transitions from out there
To the personal, private place
Horseshoes hung above
Talismans buried beneath
Mirrors behind to deflect
Protection charms carved
Hexes hung high
Lamb's blood painted lintels
Rice or seed scattered to delay
Salt an unbroken barrier
Dogs bark to warn
An instinctual pause
When a knock sounds at a door
An internal investigation,
a battle between
Curiosity and caution
Careful who's welcomed in
There are rules evil obeys

On the Bones of the Sacrificed

On the bones of the sacrificed
Are many bridges built
Within the walls of well-born homes
Charms are often hidden
Shoes secured in chimneys,
Stuffed under floorboards, too
Or sealed within wide walls
For fertility and protection
Live animals boarded up
Secured a safe structure
For those who dwell or visit

*Archaeologists look for amulets of protection from the Mesopotamian city states and find many "skeletons," literal and symbolic, denoting the sacrifices made in many cultures to erect fine structures.

Boo Hag

Paint your dwelling haint blue
To keep the Boo Hag at bay
Or she might sneak in and steal
What you value

Hang a broom by your door
Sweep away bad intentions
Or she might sup on the breath
Of your family

Write psalms in the corners
To keep the hags from changing
You into a mount to be
At night ridden

Sprinkle cayenne and salt
Because the Boo Hag is sly
Makes you disobedient
And brings trouble

Clutch a cross while you sleep
And pray for great wisdom
For Boo Hags are tricky
And change their skin

*My introduction to the Boo Hag was the MG novel *Root Magic* by Eden Royce, the inspiration for this piece.

Anti-Semitic Association

Large noses and peaked “jew hats”
Identify a witch, indeed
“Horns under their curls”
Disguised demonic reference
Even the term “Sabbath” was used
To link the witch with Judaism

*Some point to the similarities between stereotypically Jewish “traits” and witchcraft

Brewing Trouble

Cats and cauldrons, Hats and brooms
Sure symbols of witchcraft
But first Brewer's tools of the trade
Absconded by rivals

Cats kept rodents from the grain
Grain was used for brewing
Beer brewed in cauldrons over flame
Flames burned many a witch

Tall hats marked beer making gals
Gals were often "witches"
Witches used to fly on their brooms
Brooms set outside meant beer

*German beer making guilds rarely admitted women into their membership, so to alert potential patrons when a batch of beer was ready, tall-hat-wearing beer-brewing women would set their brooms outside their doors.

Homey Things

Knives for many purposes
Not only cut - also direct
Broomsticks made for cleaning
Preempted for moonlit flights
Cauldrons cooking homey stews
Embrace and blend the sweetest spells
Pins and needles to hold and sew
Bind or harm or heal with intent
Twine and string secures things
Woven into wonderous witchery

Witching Hour

Be it moonlit midnight or
The dark of three am
(that hour thought to mock
The Holy Trinity)
The devils' hour calls
A siren song of spells
When witches' wisdom wins
Wild wishes whirl with wings
Through active and subconscious

Wise Spirit

Merge masculine and feminine
Energies all
Creative visualization
Set intention
Hear the voices
of the silence
Inner wisdom
Outward guides
Connected spirit of all things

White Witchery

Healers and helpers
Cunning women, charming gals
Menders and finders
Fonts of wisdom, keeping peace

Black Craft

Harm inflicted on others
Bring illness, famine, fire
Blight the community
Curses cast for vengeance
Selfish seeking

Tools of the Trade

Cup and Cauldron
Wand and bell
Used to make
The witches' spell

Altar and incense
Pentacle
Plied to find
The witches' soul

Rods and pendants
Talking board
Enriches what
The witches hoard

Rope and clothing
Salt and skull
Found to aid
The witches' call

Candles and crystals
Athame
Channel what
The witches' see

Mirror and cards
Book and knife
Tools used in
The witches' life

Kijo

Resentment and hard living
Twist and taint a woman's spirit
Until her karma transforms
Her into grotesque Oni

*In Japan, fetus-munching Kijo (or Onibaba "Demon Hags" for the elderly) haunt folk and fairy tales such as "The Legend of Momiji."

Maiden, Mother, Crone

A trio of aspects
Glowing within women
Each taking precedence
At the appointed time
Yet all living within
Every feminine soul

Foxy Ladies

Able to shape shift,
Become invisible,
Possess another's soul,
And cast an illusion,
foxes make powerful allies

Kitsune-mochi
The solitary witch
Lures a fox into service
With promises of food
In exchange for service

Tsukimono-suji-
Hereditary witch-
Inherit foxy friends
From their witchy mothers-
Considered contagious

*Tsukimono-suji, or fox-witch families of Japan, are respected for their powers, but they're often shunned and feared for fear of "contagion." To this day, property owned by such families is often difficult to sell, and young women from the families sometimes find it difficult to date and marry.

Hidden People

Beneath the ground or among the rocks
Dwell many Hidden Folk
Underground people, trolls, dwarves, and elves
Whose origins are thus:
Those who fell to rooftops and the fields
When the angels rebelled
Made homes in waterways and the woods
within Germanic lands
Absorbed into nature, becoming land
Spirits not for or against the Fallen -
Or
Eve hid some of her children from God's gaze
Embarrassed by her lust
She hid them from God, He hid them from her
Invisible to men
Mischievous spirits dwelling with men
Incorporeal sometimes
Capable of great deeds or much harm
Capricious as the winds
Much like their brethren of the British lands
The Summerland Fair Folk

Weaker Vessel

Susceptible to outward influences
Frailer, too, in frame
Given little authority
To them the devil came

Not educated, so "of weaker mind"
Infantilized, oft'
Given little agency
To them the devil came

*In most areas, and by review of most recorded reports, women historically made up around 80 percent of deaths due to conviction of witchcraft.

Braids

She braids protections into her hair
With each twist she adds a prayer
Threaded through with black thread
Crystal beads and amethyst
Captured intentions like spring dew
On a freshly opened rose

*Many cultures use braids and embellishments to focus intention, promote healing, and provide protection.

Cooking up Spells

Cradle of creation
Reminiscent of the womb
Filled with potential
To heal or for the tomb

Conveyor of components
Needed for the craft
Ensnarer of incantations
From last until first draft

*The cauldron, like many homey things, are often associated with witchcraft.

Countercharms

Rhymes and prayers,
Hand motions
Sign of cross,
Colorful strings,
Blessed beads,
Holy waters,
Special stones
Ways to walk
Sew charms into clothing
Braid into hair
Like pirates did
Against drowning
And Vikings
Against injury
And safe return
Carve into buildings
Hide in architecture
Love protection
In wedding traditions
Hagstones, horseshoes
Boil pins in milk
of bewitched cow
Bags, bones, herbs
Hold breath, close eyes
Spitting spells

*Countercharms are supposed to protect people from harmful magic, yet aren't they a form of magic on their own?

Bath

Pre Roman occupation
People worshiped at a spring
A tri-aspected goddess called Sulis
Who the Romans associated
With their goddess Minerva
And likewise used the spring
For prophesy
And as a place of healing
To this day people come
To enjoy the healing water

*Sacred Springs at Bath, England

Island of Witches

Drink from the spring
Sprung from within
The roots of the
Ancient Balete Tree
Wellspring of magic
Whispers of old
Where creatures
Cavort with witches

*Siquijor, Philippines, called The Island of Witches by its Spanish colonizers, continues its tradition of magical healers (mananambal) and hexers (mambabarang)

Isle of Blakulla

Use good sense,
Visitor,
And don't steal from
Bla Jungfrun Island

Its rocks intrigue,
bewitch,
Its pathways wind
Through ancient labyrinths

On prehistoric altars,
archaeologists,
Discovered evidence
Of pagan rituals

On this isle where,
Once,
Witches flew to celebrate
Their festivals

*Many who visit Bla Jungfrun Island National Park, Sweden, leave offerings. Bad luck befalls those who steal from the island. All visitors must leave before nightfall.

Hellenismos

Magisses
Have their work
In ancient times and now
Spell sayers, prayer producers:
Epoida
Creator of curse tablets:
Katadesmoi
Poison and potion promoters:
Pharmaka
Amulet accusation and distribution:
Periapta
Provider of powerful love potions:
Philtra

*Hellenismos is the modern reconstruction of ancient Greek religious practices.

Appalachian Annie

Mind your footing when you hike
Along Appalachian trails
If you see stone and wood circles
Leave them alone
Don't disturb the symbols carved
Into the nearby trees
or run your fingers along
Spirals carved in stone
Ignore the whispering wind
That seems to know your name
And the crying of women and babies
There's much in ancient mountains
To be feared and left alone
Some mothered by a witch
The folk call Annie
So stick to assigned paths
And be safely tucked in bed
Before night descends
Shake the dust off of your shoes
Before you go inside
Say your prayers and hope
You escaped Annie's attention
Because her kindred enjoy
Following the unsuspecting
To torment them anew
In their homes

Granny Magic

Appalachian Mountain Mommas
Tying knots and speaking spells
Watching seasons, finding rhythms
Balance in all things does well

Moon-eyed minglers from vast cultures
Embraced by the mountain ways
Mawmaw led, chillin' learnin'
Here the folksy wisdom stays

When Fog Rolls Down the Mountain

When fog rolls down the mountain
When blue dances in the flame
When cold settles like a cloak
On a sunny afternoon
When familiar smells linger
Like a distant memory
Invisible eyes watch then
A ghostly menagerie

Signs of a Haunt

Chills and shivers wrack the bones
Pets unreasoned whimper, howl
Babies babble, reach, and point
At nothing in the distance
Creaks, footfalls in empty rooms
Knocks, strange noises, and odd smells
Icy breezes and cold spots
Voices quite disembodied
Things go missing or return

Charlemagne

Charlemagne did not believe in witchcraft
And decreed those who would execute
A person for witchcraft would instead
Be put to death

Methodology of Protection from Witchcraft

The Inquisition sought repentance
restoration of the soul
Would often "forgive" a first offense
No more "heresy" meant life

Catholics kept a holy arsenal
Exorcism and the like
Prayers for intercession by the saints
Protections placed throughout homes

Protestant beliefs disarmed themselves
No countercharms were allowed
Leaving no recourse but "civil trials"
A burnt and bloody path left

This Thomas Didn't Doubt

In Thomas Acquinas' time there was a
Belief in harmful magic
Which was punishable by death
And spiritual "apostasy"
Which was legal
And held that a witch possessed no
Malevolent powers but instead
Succumbed to "Illusions of
Diabolical agency."
Thomas had another idea
And combined these beliefs
To assert witchcraft was blasphemy
And evil minded and therefore
Punishable by death-
Which became the basis for
Many witchcraft laws.

Aquinas studied Aristotle
Who believed, because of menstruation,
Women were inferior to men
And it was through a man's semen
That the soul was passed
These two men, great and lasting thinkers,
Further believed Women's bodies polluted men
And their menstrual blood "uncanny"
And able to cause great harm
Thomas the supposed saint
Through his study and belief
In Aristotle's sexist philosophy
Influenced many laws and
Thereby helped to facilitate
The numerous witch trials
Of the early modern time-
And even some today

*Thomas Acquinas (1225-1275 AD)

Some Witchcraft Laws in Great Britain (that informed the colonies)

1541 Henry VIII of England was the first to formally define witchcraft as a felony, which is a crime punishable by death and the forfeiture of goods and chattels

1562 Elizabeth I of England passed an act against conjurations, witchcrafts, and enchantments, which allowed lesser offenses without loss of life to be punished with a jail term (instead of automatic death)

1563 Mary Queen of Scots decreed "no person take upon hand to use any matter of witchery…"

1586 Irish Witchcraft Act was nearly identical to the English 1562 Act. (It was repealed in 1821)

1603 James I expanded witchcraft penalties with An Act Against Conjuration, Witchcraft, and Dealing With Evil and Wicked Spirits

1649 Scottish extension of previous witchcraft act that included the death penalty for those who deal with or consult devils and familiar spirits

1735 Great Britain changed the focus to "penalties for the pretense of witchcraft"

1736 English penalties for witchcraft shifted from death to fines for those claiming magical practices and activities

1951 Fraudulent Mediums Act replaced the former Acts in Great Britain. This was repealed in 2008 by the Consumer Protection Regulations.

*1985 The District Court of Virginia, USA, declared Wicca a religion with religious protection

Around the World:

*Saudi Arabia, Cameroon, and South Africa have official legislation against witchcraft.
*1957 The Witchcraft Suppression Act of South Africa is based on the 1735 Act and is still in effect.

Witches in Literature and Media

Witches as Art

Witches fly alongside
An illuminated writing,
One on a broom, wearing red,
The other a gown of gold
Rides a stick
In Martin le France's page
From Ladies' Champion from 1451

Albrecht Durer carved woodcuts
From when old hag witches
Rode backwards on goats
To witches' sabbaths
Flipping the natural order
Lusty, unbridled, holding a broom
Old or young, naked as a child
Newborn into a world as warning

Durer's eager apprentice
Hans Baldung Grien in 1510
Created provocative pieces
With whole covens depicted
Cackling around a cauldron
Naked, twisted, sexy,
To the patriarchy terrifying

Frans Francken in 1606
Painted a chaotic scene
With two women at the center
Of a demon summoning
Spell ingredients and a circle
Tell the story of their act

Engravings in pamphlets
Exploited deep rooted fears
Depicting wicked women
Performing evil deeds
Described in trials
Making the horrors accessible
For even the illiterate

Matthew Hopkins,
Self-proclaimed Witchfinder General
Commissioned an aggrandizing image
With himself in the center
Of two witches' tableaux
Where the old ladies name
Their many familiars for his book
The Discovery of Witches in 1647

Goya made the witch a metaphor
Conjured from the recesses of
A satirical imagination
Bristling with stereotypes
Naked withered hags

Salvatore Rosa marks a turning point
Depicting incredulity through
Almost farcical stereotyped imagery
Dark skies and corpse-light skin
Demons cavorting with skeletons
Baby sacrifice and hung man's toes
Bird-headed beings at a sabbath
Provide his many witchy scenes

Henry Fuseli
Portrayed the Weird Sisters
From Shakespeare's Scottish play
With theatrical flair
Witches inhabit corners of dreams
Pull mandrakes from pots

William Blake channels
The Whore of Babylon
Surreal and lurid
Astride her many-headed mount
And crowns Triple Hecate
In the late seventeen hundreds

Nineteenth century witches
Found reinterpretation by
The Pre Raphaelite schools
Femme-fatale allusions
To classical antiheroines
From Frederick Sandys
And Evelyn De Morgan

To John William Waterhouse
Beautifully pushing the witch into
The realm of fantasy and fiction

Goudie was possessed
By the spirit of a witch
Named Nanny
And portrayed her
In his paintings many times
Never able to exorcise
Her hold on his imagination
Pale skin, ruby lips, often nude

Thomas Satterwhite Noble's
Witch Hill imagines a maid
Convicted by her neighbors and
uses as a model the granddaughter of
A woman hung during the Salem situation

Fairytale artists Arthur Rackham and Ivan Bilibin
With their dreamy interpretations of traditional tales
Erna Rosenstein (who self-identifies as a fairy witch)
Kay Nielsen with flights of fancy
Disney Studio artists took a turn
Shaping suppositions and interpretations
Kinuko Y. Craft with luminous landscapes
Etienne Delessert with watercolored whimsy
Paul Zelinski called on Renaissance inspiration

Modern interpretations range from
Campy, like Andy Warhol's The Witch
And Jakki Moore's cartoony Wine Witch
Or whimsical takes like those by Rene Biertempfl
And Molly Harrison feel nostalgic
Earnest Gothic inspires Andrew Kwit
Sympathetic or unhinged
(to name but a few)

Photographic display from Peabody
Carolee Schneeman in the 1960's
Virginia Lee Montgomery
Clothing by the same

*Inspired by Exhibition, Depictions of the Witch Through Art, Edinburgh National Gallery, Scotland and The Peabody, Salem

Underworld Overseer

Sense magic in the boundaries
At liminal transitions
Tri-facing goddess of witchcraft
Mysterious night mama
Wise as wonder, grave as ghosts
By her dog pack protected
Necromantic harvest friend
With cold torches, keys, and knives
In Grecian art depicted
Emitting darkness in the light
Soothing serpents and lions
Maiden, mother, crone in one
Mysterious as the new moon
When best to leave an off'ring

*For Hecate, Greek goddess of magic and witchcraft (She's often depicted as a three faced woman carrying a torch or pair of serpents, or three women, back to back like a pillar.)

Necromantic Endor

In disguise, cloaked with night,
The first Hebrew King sought her aid

"Why should I help you who've killed my kind?
Should I believe you've not entrapped me?
For though Hammurabi's Code tolerates,
Your Hebrew God condemns us."

Saul swore by his God no harm would befall her
And begged her to summon a prophet

Through necromancy, Samuel appeared
Divine being sprung from the ground
Saul cowered and trembled in true terror
His face bowed low against the floor

Saul begged for guidance from the spirit
What against the Philistines should he do?

He'd not completed God's tasks before
So Saul and his sons would die in battle

David, who he hated, would be the next king
Samuel left Saul in despair

This woman called witch bade Saul then to sit
Killed and cooked her fatted calf and baked bread

She asked nothing for payment, but fed them
instead
And one wonders how did they know her?
If all of the region was cleansed of magic,
How was this woman alive?

*Inspired by 1 Samuel and these passages in the Old Testament of the Bible
"No practicing divination or soothsaying." Leviticus 19:26
"You shall not suffer a witch to live." Exodus 22:18
"A medium or spiritist shall surely be put to death." Leviticus 20:27
"As for the person who turns to mediums or spiritists, I shall set my face against them and will cut them off from their people." Leviticus 20:6
"Do not seek out spiritists, for you will be defiled by them." Leviticus 19:31
Deuteronomy 17:18-19 & 18:9-12

Medea

Ancient bad butt
Embraced by Greek gods
Not to be trifled with
As evidenced by her myth

Went against her father
Charmed a dragon guard
To claim the Golden Fleece
For marriage in Greece

To a would-be hero
Who couldn't accomplish
Any of his heroic acts
Without her magic - FACTS!

When her foolish husband
Tried to cast her aside
Her ire and indignation
Proved his ruination

Rival

Princess perfect
Loved shiny things
Even a husband
Made shiny by gold fleece
she acquired for him
Through charm and wit
And murderous blood
Gifted a concession
Presented by her sons
A shiny crown
And sun-bright gown
Laced with something special
A spell
A poison
To kill not only her
But those nearby

*For Medea, of Helios' blood, from the Ancient Greek Argonautica and Euripides' titular tragedy.

Done Wrong

For a husband's failure
To sacrifice the Cretan Bull
To Poseidon of the sea,
Pasiphae the wife queen
Was cursed to fall in love
With that self-same bull,
Climb into a creation
Of Daedalus inventor,
A hollow cow, and mate
Conceive, and bear
The murderous Minotaur.

Displeased with the turn of events
And in light of King Minos' Infidelities,
Pasiphae cursed her husband
To ejaculate snakes, scorpions,
And centipedes
Whenever he laid with another,
Killing any concubine.

*For Pasiphae, Queen of Crete, daughter of Helios and Perse, worshipped as an oracle, celestial goddess, and adroit magic user.

Night

Black-robed goddess
Cloak of night
Child of Chaos
And Darkness
Bringer of sleep
Afeared by Zeus
Revered by witches

*For Nyx, also of Ancient Greek Mythology

Hosted Odysseus

She
Fed his men which
Turned them into pigs
Took Odysseus in
And bore him three sons
Before offering life-saving advice
She
Restored his men
To human form
And bid the hero safe passage

*Inspired by Circe of Ancient Greek Mythology, the daughter of the sun god Helios and the sea nymph Perse or the goddess Hecate- it's hard to say for certain, since she was born a long ago.

Transformation

Born of divinity
She
Lived by her own terms
On the Isle of Aeaea
In a stone mansion
With a great throne
From which she ruled
Great beasts, all tame
As her housepets
With nymphs for servants

Unlucky in love
She
Was infatuated with
Gallant Glaucous
Who was smitten with
Another who
She
Gave a potion
Which transformed his gal
Into a great sea monster
She
Fell for the son of Chronos
Picus by name
But he also loved another
She
changed him into
A jaunty woodpecker

Thessalian Necromantic

Dark night spirit speaker
Creeps out on starless eves
Serpent girded spellcaster
Whose breath poisons the air
Hades-raising woman
Stinking of burnt flesh
Invading tombs
Copulating corpses
Consuming carrion
Unrestrained evil
indiscriminate attack
Sublime subjugation
Extract organs
Harvest with own hands
Steal and use children
Corrupt their innocence
Their very blood and body
Ripping embryos
From wombs quick and dead
For their fearsome spells
Raising soulless servants
From forgotten flesh

*Inspired by Ericthro as described by Lucan
Pharsalia, 61AD

Mesopotamian Fears

Little hands,
Long fingered,
Filthy elbowed,
Ingratiate themselves
Though feigned friendship
With pregnant women
Count days until delivery
Worm her way through
Locks secured
Enter nurseries to
Nurse heirs with poison
Or steal girls as pupils
Or simply Kill the little ones

From 1200BC and 12BC

Theoris of Lemnos

Three accredited, ancient sources
Philochorus
Demosthenes
And Plutarch
Described the witchcraft trial of Theoris of Lemnos

This woman is described by them as
A seer
A Witch or druggist
And a priestess
Who was convicted for the crimes of either
Impiety
Casting incantations and harming with drugs
Or teaching slaves to deceive

Though they differ in the details, they all agree
There was a woman named Theoris of Lemnos
Charged with using magic before 323 BC
And she and her children were executed

Strix

Oh nightmare!
Screeching in the evening
You take on any form
Seemingly innocent
To access any place
Especially those forbidden
Enchant guards to sleep
Oh Strigga!
Created by evil spells
Old women into birds
Flying, deformed women
Suck out infant innards
Sup on decayed flesh

*Inspired by ancient Greek legends illustrating fears of necromantic, shape-shifting, child-stealing witches as interpreted by Ovid, 8AD and Apuleius, 170AD

Heka

Complicated family trees
With roots twisted upon themselves,
Where brother tricks brother
And only by a sister-wife's wit,
With help from their sister
Who was married to the murderer,
is saved, but not the same
And this darker sister bears
The jackal-headed god of embalming

*The Egyptian goddess Isis invoked magic for healing and protection, as did her sister, Nephthys, the goddess of mourning, death, and decay, who could raise the dead, protect the deceased during their journey through the underworld, and yet could still heal if the mood struck her.
*Heka was the ancient Egyptian word for magic, which involved manipulating the natural and supernatural realms, but it was also the name of their god of magic and medicine. Magic threaded through all aspects of ancient Egyptian life, death, and afterlife.

Mexican Siren

Long, wavy hair the essence of midnight
Starlight glinting in alluring eyes
Seductive dress pale as yucca flower
Skimmed over voluptuous curves
With the tinkling voice of the alluring
She calls from behind the casaba tree
To lure unwary men into the jungle

Uma of the Andes

High up in the Andes
It's best to take care-
Betrayed by her beloved
La Uma seeks revenge
Staring with bulging eyes
Gnashing dagger teeth,
Her long, tangled hair
Streaming like a black flag
Of vengeance
This clever witch
Curses with a sweet voice
Pursuing unwary men
By pulling off her head
Twisting between his legs,
Bewildering and tripping him
Until he plunges to his death

*Some families in Peru still keep cacti on their windowsill to protect against La Uma's vengeance, since she becomes tangled in brambles and branches.

Freyja

Flaxen haired goddess
Named the last workday
Magic, gold-teared beauty
With a cat-pulled chariot
Adorned with falcon feather cloak

*Freyja is the Norse goddess of beauty, love, fertility, war, gold, & magic
*Freya's chariot was probably pulled by boars, not cats, but the image was too good.

Swamp Jenny

A young girl at play
Lost her hoop in a marsh
Reaching with a stick,
Balanced precariously
To hook the toy,
She strained but
It floated further
in the murky water
She stretched, swayed,
Not noticing the
Algae-covered arms
Of the famished swamp witch
Come to claim her prize

*Jenny Greenteeth is sometimes a fairy creature, sometimes a swamp witch, but always a cautionary tale warning children away from dangerous waterways.

Maternal Magic

What wouldn't a mother do
To secure her children's happiness?
A magic potion she might brew
And give to a married man
His mind it would confuse
Until he forgot his vows
And marry a mother's girl, Gudrun
Which frees the forgotten bride
So a mother's son could then woo
Then both children would be wed
That something Grimhild might pursue.

*This is inspired by a bit of the story of Sigurd and his bride, Brynhilde.
Grimhild wanted to find good matches for her children, Gudrun and Gunnar. She thought Sigurd and Brynhilde would make a perfect son- and daughter-in-law. Who cares that they were happily married to one another? Well, certainly not Grimhild or her progeny.

Great Chase

Run, wise Taliesin, recently reborn
Put your poetic mind to work
Ceridwen pursues you
for the wisdom you've stolen
From her brewing cauldron
You transform into a hare
But she snaps greyhound jaws
Upon your fluffy white tail
You dive into a lake
Turned into a fish
But she swims with ease
As a lithe otter
You burst from the water
Reach for the sky
The wings of wren lift you
But her shrill shriek
Warns she's a hawk in pursuit
You disguise yourself as corn
Golden and plump
Perfect for her as a hen
To devour
You must make amends
For the potion you wrecked
Made for Morfran, the son of
This Welsh witch of rebirth,
Transformation, and inspiration

*Ceridwen's dispute with the poet Taliesin is found in the 12th century works by Gogynfeirdd (and other sources).

Scottish Spellwork

Round about the cauldron they
Three sisters wise as break of day
Toss into their charmed black pot
Ingredients enchanted
To cast a spell both far and wide
From penny-paid to royal side
That shocks and awes the theatre
Scottish Play eternal
When double, double toil and trouble
Steal the show with potion's bubble
And worm their way into the minds
Of Spectators enchanted
Round about the cauldron go
They make the feeling of the show
With hex and curse fortelling
Three witches win the words

*Inspired by William Shakespeare's marvellous three witches' spellwork from *MacBeth* (or The Scottish Play)

On William Shakespeare's *MacBeth*

I hope you'll forgive my nod to The Bard's immortal work. Who can compare to his incomparable poetry? Certainly not me. Yet I couldn't leave his "weird sisters" from this. They're a part of my interpretation of the subject, because they're so cool.

Incidentally, did you know the word "weird" gained popularity because of this play?

Speaking of odd, many actors hold the superstitious belief that it's bad luck to say the name of the play itself aloud. Instead, they call it "The Scottish Play." If the name is mistakenly said aloud, there's a complicated banishing ritual to be done to dispel the ill luck. Witchery! Fun!

If you have the chance to see this play live, the appearance of the weird sisters feels like witnessing live spellwork. It's magical! And their speech is so different from Shakespeare's regular writing that it sets them quite apart.

Here's a breakdown on some of the spell ingredients the witches used in their recitation, according to Dictionary.com:

Renaissance and Medieval herbalists and apothecaries would use fanciful names for their products. So, to the best of scholars' guesses:

"Eye of Newt" would be mustard seed. ("Eye" referred to the seeds of the plant.)
"Toe of Frog" would be the bulbous buttercup.
"Tongue of Dog" would be the toxic plant houndstongue.
"Adder's Fork" would be the trout lily.
"Lizard's Leg" is thought to be ivy, since it's green and climbs up trees.
"Scale of Dragon" could be either the dragon's scale plant or tarragon.
"Tooth of Wolf" could be either the plants wolves' bane or club moss.
"Blind Worm's Sting" could be poppy seed, knotwood, or wormwood.
"Root of Hemlock digg'd i' the dark" would be hemlock, a poisonous plant.
"Wool of Bat" could be either moss or holly leaves. (Or maybe it really was a snip of bat fur.)
"Maw and Gulf of the ravin'd salt-sea shark" could also be an accurate description.
"Witch's Mummy" most likely was an accurate description, since contemporary people believed witches ate powdered, mummified remains, usually found in bogs.
"Fillet of Fenny Snake" could be either the plants Jack-in-the-pulpet or snakeroot or real leeches

Witchcraft in Your Lips

Bright ruler of Egypt proud
Beloved, adored by e'ery crowd
About whom only tainted sources
Wrote felonious discourses
Cleopatra, live out loud!

*First hand accounts of Cleopatra's reign burned when we lost the library at Alexandria. Historians who wrote of her after these lost, primary sources attributed most of her accomplishments to her sexuality and even accused her of using magic to achieve her goals, instead of crediting her with a powerful intellect and political acumen.

Genesis of the Malleus Maleficarum

Seven women, Helena in the lead,
Put on trial for witchcraft
With one superstitious woman-hater
As the lead prosecutor
Papal appointed
Power hungry
Helena defended and represented
Put prosecutor Kramer to shame
Which inspired him to write his book
And postulate a suspected witch
Should be tortured immediately and
Allowed no legal representation

*This blatantly misogynistic book was written after Heinrich Kramer's papal-granted authority was questioned at this trial, and he was laughed at. In this book, he expressly disallowed the interference of an attorney or legal representation and encouraged the immediate torture of the suspected witches to extract confessions. It was originally published in 1486.

A Damning Book

Michael Dalton
Wrote a book -
The Country Justice -
Published in 1618,
Though oft' reprinted,
Which provided
Guidance for judges and
Justices of the Peace
Of English common law
Which included guidelines
For witchcraft allegations
Emphasizing the search
Of bodies for evidence
Of demonic contact-
Witches' teats -
And brutalizing those
Assumed guilty

The Midnight Hour

The midnight stillness shattered
The dead restless grow
Invisible assailants
Their malicious magics show
Uprooting righteous beginnings
Witch reunions glow
Like baleful moonbright beacons
To which initiates go

*Inspired by John Greenleaf Whittier's poem "The Weird Gathering," 1831, which was itself influenced by Cotton Mather's reflections on the witch trials.

A Stone's Throw

It started with injustice
As many of these tales do
An elderly widow without name-
In that she had a name,
But the teller of the tale
Didn't think it important
enough to even record it-
Done wrong by a George Walton
Who stole her land as his own
To build a tavern and lodging,
Called upon an ancient being,
A spirit of the very earth
Called Lithobolia, the stone-thrower,
Who did his job, hurling projectiles
All through many nights
And like a good poltergeist,
Tossed about home goods, too
Causing dismay, fright, and even
The occasional bodily injury

Until the Waltons and guests
Peed in a pot filled with pins
And set it over a fire to harm
The witch who harmed them -
But the joke was on them,
Because Lithobolia the invisible
Broke their pot before the
Countercharm did its work

*Inspired by a short narrative, Lithobolia by Richard Chamberlayne, written in 1698 though described earlier, that added to a lot of the fears in New England, including those experienced in Salem, Massachusetts during their infamous witch hunt.

Making a Man

Old Mother Rigby
Would make a new man
And dress him in fine clothes
No mere scarecrow was he
Nor hobgoblin
But a marvel, indeed, to behold
She used for his spine
a broomstick
Meal bags created his girth
For his head
she painted a pumpkin
And declared him
The finest on earth
With his coat of fine, gilded velvet
And his feathered, tri-cornered hat
He mirrored the colors of autumn
and resembled the greatest of men
She called on invisible Dicken
And bade him light up her pipe
Which danced with amber-hued demons
And conveyed to her toy a new life
He charmed pretty maid Polly
But he soon recognized within
He was not real but a strawman
And repented a life full of sin

*A nod to "Feather Top" by Nathaniel Hawthorne (1852)

Aradia Gospel

Teaching the downtrodden
Secret spells
To use against oppressors
Central to the witches' rites
Of some modern pagan times
Embraced by Raven Grimassi
Ash, Birch, and Willow tree
New tradition in Italy

*Inspired by the 1899 work by Charles Godfrey Leland

Candy Coated

Lured by sugar
Spun with words
Willed into an oven
Baked by dinner
Screamed with sticks
Burned into another

*Inspired by the Grimm tale of "Hansel and Gretel"

Goodman

Unleashed in primeval forest
A goodman followed a path
Left behind his Faith, bound in ribbons
Turn back, young man, turn back.

Met a mysterious stranger
A dark man in a black hat
"To thee is this sinful world given"
Turn back, young man, turn back.

Multitudes of good town people
natives intent on the kill
State secrets to take dark communion
Turn back, young man, turn back.

Hypocrisy and hidden sin
Snake sticks, inherited crime
"You'll think better of this by and by"
Turn back, young man, turn back.

*Taking inspiration from Nathaniel Hawthorne's excellent short story, "Young Goodman Brown" (1835)

May Queenly

Upon her spring-soft head
They crown her with flowers
To lead the festivities
That often last for hours

Dance with ribbons round a pole
Phallic symbolization
Join king and queen together
For future civilization

Embodiment of earth
Pure potential to explore
By crowning personified
good harvests do assure

*Inspired by Alfred, Lord Tennyson's poem "The May Queen" and Molly Smith Meltzler's play of the same name.
*This may be more witch-adjacent, but it felt like something to include in this collection.

Mrs. Mothersole

She couldn't escape the hangman's noose
She uttered a curse before it grew tight
"There will be guests at the hall"
Her accuser died within a fortnight

*Inspired by The Ash Tree by M. R. James, 1904

Witches Conjure

Come to the cabin to see them
Their woodfire sparks in the night
Spirits sing silvered cantations
The children all shiver with fright

Come at the sister's dark calling
Ignore the black cat's frantic plea
Enrich their magical powers
From limitations be finally free

*Dedicated to the Sanderson Sisters of Salem, 1693-1993 (Winnifred, Sarah, and Mary Sanderson are fictional characters from the fantastic nostalgia film, "Hocus Pocus," 1993.)
*First published in *Death Wish Poetry* Magazine, Issue 4, Resurrection, 2025.

Witch Through a Wardrobe

You claim to be a human
As you rule the wintry land
With crystal crown atop you
And snowy, frost-firm hand

But in truth you are the white witch
Part frost giant and part jinn
With a strangle-hold on Narnia
Assured you'll always win

Yet you fear the sons of Adam
And daughters of Eve, too
Because they can wake Aslan
Which means the end of you

*Inspired by C.S. Lewis's wicked White Witch of Narnia, published in aspects of the Chronicles of Narnia, 1950-1956.

Willing Witchery

Serving special sugar
With the blackberries
That grow as wild
As savages raised
In ancestral castles
With subtext unsaid
Blended perfectly
haunting designs
Willing witchery
Into the everyday

*For Shirley Jackson, who I would have hoped would be a friend.

Sisters

Stars shine within and gleam without
A midnight margarita eve
Enchanted winds and love-lorn men
All to the garden gate they cry
Aunties dance and children caper
Spectral beetles tick and warn
Herbal nosegays perfume power
Cursed in love but not forsworn
tangled in the family trauma
Girls who capture living sighs
Glow within unleashed enchantment
Sisters love never compromised

*Using for inspiration Alice Hoffmann's most enchanting novel, *Practical Magic* (1995).

East End Goddesses

Immortal but cursed
Because of trouble in Salem
Sisters hide their nature
And make do without magic
Until romance blooms
And curses crumble
To reveal an astonishing truth

*Inspired by the Witches of East End series by Melissa de la Cruz, 2011-2013

Bewitching

A beautiful opening
Dashing through a starry sky
With a wiggle of your little nose
You made fun fancies fly
Immortalized in Salem
A bronze broom astride
A flashy mother in caftans
You made a bewitching bride

*For Samantha, Endora, Tabitha, and all of those who "Bewitched" me in syndication

Discovering Witches

Diana Bishop, of magical blood,
A professor researching magic tomes
-The darkest academia-
Becomes the object of affection
Of a charming vampire, Matthew
-A forbidden romance-
They team up to discover the roots
Of supernatural species
-a dangerous pursuit-

*Inspired by The All Souls Trilogy by Deborah Harkness, 2011

Upon a Turtle World

No-nonsense ladies who know the best way
To accomplish whatever needs done
Be it surviving a burning or a swim test
These magical maids show what's what
Without the panache of the wizarding school
They quietly get important things done
Using First Sight to truly see the truth
And Second Thoughts to know their own minds
E'er aware of melodrama cackling
Which warns of wicked "going to the bad"

*Discworld witches (Tiffany and Granny Aching, Nanny Ogg, Weatherwax, and the rest) by Terry Pratchett

Spellman

Appearing first in comic books
With Archie and the gang
Sabrina Spellman cast a spell
On readers cross the land
Her short white hair and winning smile
Brought fans by the dozen
Then she branched out to a series
With her cute cat Salem
She and her aunts enchanted folks
left a sweet impression
Another channel picked her up
Sent in dark directions

*Sabrina Spellman, teenaged witch of Archie comics (and her aunts) and the shows, animated, sitcommy, and serious)

Empathetic Ends

Troubled boy seeing too much
Unintentional communing
Inadvertent apocalypse
With compassionate soothing
An age-old wrong put to rights
Generational improving

*for the midnight premiere of the 2012 animated film, "ParaNorman," watched with my golden-haired beauty.

Little Witches, Big Dreams

Deep breath, head nod
New home, new job
Created by grit
Avoided pitfalls
Maintained with work
Integrity and friendship
Putting powers to good use

*Inspired by the 1989 Studio Ghibli animated film adaptation of Eiko Kadono's novel, "Kiki's Delivery Service" and the 1962 cartoon "Wendy the Good Little Witch" by Harvey Comics

Magnificent, Marvelous

Wacky and wild
Purple-haired child
Dueled with Merlin
To win a king

Broke the rules
Of magic duels
Became a dragon
But lost a king

*Inspired by the Magnificent, Marvelous, Mad Madam Mim from Disney's "Sword in the Stone" (1963) which was adapted from T.H. White's novel *Once and Future King*

Substitutiary Locomotion

Rouse the troops
Protect the kids
When WWII
antagonists
Invade England
Witch-in-training
Eglantine Price
Proves her point
With a spell

*Channeling the lovely Angela Lansbury who played Miss Eglantine Price in *Bedknobs and Broomsticks*, 1971

Grandma Witch

With a wave of your wizened hand
And a sprinkling of magic spice
You crafted curated meals
That tasted wonderous nice

But the secret to good spellcraft
Is knowing how and when to end
Three kisses in a cauldron
Will be a cook's best friend

* *Strega Nona* by Tomie dePaola is a delightfully illustrated folktale about "Grandma Witch," "Big Anthony," and her magic pot (1977)

Unabashedly Bad

They hold themselves with poise
Present a handsome face
Dress with stunning style
Walk with beauty and grace

Power brims in their skin
Magical currents combined
Yet an ingenue claims the lead
And leaves these ladies behind

*For these witchy villains who made the Disney adapted fairytales great: The Evil Queen from Snow White, Ursula the Sea Witch from Little Mermaid, Maleficent from Sleeping Beauty (although, see below…she's just too cool to leave out of this) and Mother Gothel from Rapunzel

Queen Elora Bane

In an attempt to destroy the marked child
Prophesied to one day be a queen
She expelled her mighty power
Upon Nockmaar
Transformed, enslaved,
The heroes faced their darkest hour
Willow and Fin Raziel worked unseen
Restoring order, Bavmorda's reign defiled

*Inspired by Bavmorda from the 1988 film *Willow*

Hallowitches

Into a land of Halloween
Stowed aboard an occult bus
To embrace a heritage
Of magic forbidden

*Inspired by the Cromwell witches of
Halloweentown, 1998

Bellflower

The oldest of the European Fables
Captured within comic pages
Known by many a name
Ms Child Killer, the Black Forest Witch,
Oft has her own hid'n agenda
Her help comes with a price

*Frau Totenkinder is a character from D.C. comics created by Bill Willingham

Crisis in a Mortar and Pestle

Boney legged Grandmama
In your Russian wood
Head wrapped in a babushka
Teeth an iron grin
Keeping guests to a minimum
With boney-skull-grin fence
Around your so distinctive
Chicken leg cottage
Turning foes to feathered pets
Or eating annoyances
Especially succulent babes
Unless they win your fickle favor

*Baba Yaga figures in many Slavic, Romanian, and Serbo-Croatian tales.

Witchcraft Through the Ages

Sympathetic exploration
Of times of dark torment
When superstition ruled the day
And devils harmed at night

Contrasted modern and the old
Interpretations made
When tortured, murdered in the past
Modern doctors help today

*For the Swedish silent film *Haxan* (1922)
sympathetic "exploration" and "Documentary."

Pyewacket's Princess

College rivalry revenge
Unworthy, though, in truth
And why must magical women
Give up what makes them
If they fall in love with a man?

*From *Bell Book and Candle*, 1958

Oh, Snap Snap

Creepy, kooky, family fun
With witchy matriarchs
And the greatest love affair
Bar none
Mysterious and spooky
Multimedia
Mother, lover, in control
Ideal
Cultured, creative, and ooky
Multilingual songstress
Fencer, gardener, fem fatale
Cara mia

*Inspired by Morticia Addams, created by Chaz Addams (cartoon first published in the New Yorker, 1938, adapted for television, screen, and stage.)

Asa Ascended

Spiked metal mask
Pierced youthful skin
Flames lick and leap

Unpredicted
Rain
Falls

Unleash the curse
Undying wrath
Ancestral pain

*Inspired by Barbara Steele as Asa Vajda from the Italian film *Black Sunday* (1960)

Mother's Love and Father's Eyes

A woman's love
A husband's ambition
A new home in a New York brownstone

New neighbors' care
New pregnancy cravings
New revelations for a new mom

***Rosemary's Baby* by Ira Levin, 1967 (film, 1968)

Children at Play

Call the friends together
Join their hands in play
Grow demonic fur spots
To a devil pray

Led by a bright Angel
Lured to murder and rape
Rebuild the dark master
Unleash a new hellscape

*Inspired by the cult-classic 1971 folk horror film, *Blood on Satan's Claw*

Harm None

Outcasts all together
Perfect compass points
Calling on the elements
Calling on the corners
A coven creation
Magic unrestrained
Invite the power inside
Invite the power in
Moral discrepancy
Undone, broke apart
Bound from harming others
Bound from harming self

*Inspired by the 1996 film, *The Craft* because “We are the weirdos…”

Unexpected intimacy

A bit of experimentation
A spell of play
Led to a love affair
To last 'til end of days
The scent of sweet strawberries
The sip of golden honey
A swirl of all that is darkness
Mixed with the sunny

*For Willow and Tara from *Buffy the Vampire Slayer* tv show (1997-2003)

Magic in Movement

Visceral visual onslaught
Toe shoes laced up tight
Maggots falling from the ceiling
Rituals born in blood

*Inspired by the film *Suspiria* (1977 and 2018).

Bayou Voodoo

Unreliable witness
Willing disbelief
Family in flames

Alcohol-fanned attack
Enraged sister seeks
A paternal curse

Accursed infidelity
Spell brings tragedy
Truth is discovered

*The amazing Aunt Mozelle and her beautiful niece, Eve, from the 1997 film *Eve's Bayou* inspired this piece

Charmed Ones

From a lineage of magic
It was foretold
Three (and a half) sisters
would bond together
Despite differences
To fight the forces of evil
With the charmed power of three

*Inspired by the 1998 American television show *Charmed* featuring three magical Halliwell sisters.

Unseen Threat

Deep in a Maryland wood
New moon lending little light
Shivery whispers wending wide
Screams of terror shook the night

Stick strung dollies hung from trees
People pulled into the night
Naughty children in corners
From unseen witches take flight

*Inspired by the film *The Blair Witch Project*, 1999

Trio of Trouble

Three divorcees in Rhode Island
In the 1970's
Alexandra, Jane, and Sukie
Meet a horny little devil
Hilarity ensues
Until powers and pride
lead to cancerous destruction

*John Updike's 1984 novel *The Witches of Eastwick* was made into a 1987 movie with a much happier ending, television shows, and musicals.

Hazel and the Hare

Quoting Shakespearian sisters
A Misogynist Magic Mirror on her wall
An appetite for wisecracking rabbit
And chubby, cherub-like children
With an ax sharp enough to split a hare
And a soft spot for her pet spider Paul
Jealous of a Hideous Halloween mask
Brewed a "pretty potion" with a poison apple
Which she downed by accident
As a cup of tea, a cookie, and phew...
She hopped aboard her trusty broom
To escape an aggressive genie

*Witch Hazel from Loony Toons was such a fun caricature, with her delightful cackle and unashamed "ugliness."

McDuck's Dime

No withered hag you
With silky black hair
And magic through
Your supple feathers

Like Sophia Loren
You ooze appeal
But all you desire
Is a dime to steal

*Inspired by Magica De Spell from Disney's Donald Duck Comics and the *Duck Tales* animated show

Music for Mistresses

Mysterious music, messages between beats
Sinister Satanic, genealogic greet
Catastrophic concert, doomed descendants replete
Suicidal songsters, creation goal complete

*Taking as inspiration Rob Zombie's song, film, and novelization of *The Lords of Salem*

When Witches Would Win

Oh, Oz, the great and powerful
Strength rests in female hands
Who wield wild forces magically
Know they the varied lands
They see through your subterfuge
Yet let you make demands
Oh, Oz, the greatly powerless
It's witches who command

*In response to L. Frank Baum's extensive collection of Oz stories

Poor, Dead Jane

A young woman's unblemished body
Delivered to a father-son
Coroners tasked to find
The cause of her death by morning
The evidence they gather
baffles, confuses
No rigor mortis settled in her limbs
Her milky-stare eyes suggest
she'd been dead for days
With no obvious cause of death
Her wrists and ankles shattered
Her tongue cut out
And one of her molars missing
Lungs blackened burns
and sadistic smoke scars
Jimsonweed, a paralytic
in her stomach
With her tooth and
an oddly marked cloth
Spells scattered beneath her skin
Release hellish dark power

*Inspired by the 2016 horror film, *The Autopsy of Jane Doe*

What Matters

Sisters should support each other
Appearances deceive
Popular comes at a steep cost
Lonely hearts perceive

* *Wicked Musical* (2003) based on Gregory Maguire's books based on L. Frank Baum's The Wizard of Oz

For Good

Ostracized
For color
In a green world

Wickedness
Thrust upon
An innocent

Ascend high
Defend those
Without voices

*For *Wicked* in all its presentations, from book by Gregory Maguire, musical, and film, which of course are inspired by L. Frank Baum's Wonderful World.

Nice and Accurate Prophecies

Writing out prophecies in humorous truths
Sending it to the future through generations
Of wise women, culminating in Anathema
Who met the antichrist - who was a very nice lad -
Knowing the future meant knowing the end
Not only of all time but also personal,
(Though its deliverers were late by 10 minutes)
And so, loaded with fifty pounds of gunpowder
And thirty pounds of roofing nails beneath
petticoats
Agnes' burning at the stake left quite an impression

*Based on the feisty Agnes Nutter and her descendant Anathema Device from *Good Omens* by Terry Pratchett and Neil Gaiman.

Ties to the Trial

Set in Salem's Seaside town
With ports pouring fog
Descendents must break
Centuries' curse
Or history repeats

*Inspired by Adrianna Mather's *How To Hang a Witch*, 2016.

Down the Witches' Road

Streaks of crimson, royal purple
Puffs of sulfur smoke
Blackened fingers, bruised, dark hearts
Practicing the darkest arts
Internally embattled
Chaotic creation channeled

*Scarlet Witch (Wanda Maximoff) and Agatha Harkness from Marvel Comics and their television shows, *WandaVision* (2021) and *Agatha All Along* (2024)

Magical Music

Tumultuous Bohemian
With the earthy voice
Faced snowy mountains made of death
Glad she made the choice
To live and love and dance and sing
Her art to the world such joy brings

*For the talented and beautiful Stevie Nicks, who may not have been an actual witch, or maybe was.

Lucky 13

From the beginning of your career
When we thought of Tim McGraw
And it summoned images of you,
Young and curly blonde and full
Of actualized visions and ideals
We recognized you as someone
Special, magical as a sparkling
Spandex suit and thigh-high boots
The magical creator of Our Song

*For Taylor Swift, my Dylan's favorite singer, who isn't a witch to the best of my knowledge but who can "Jump from the gallows and levitate down your street..." and knows the power of imagery. Seeing her concert with Dylan and two of her friends was a treasured treat.

Mayfair Magic

Spanish moss dripping
Gnarled trees twisting shade
Plantation home columns
Flowers fall like rain
A spirit promised love
Madness caged in pills
Ancestral ages enacted
Magic to fulfill

*Based on Anne Rice's *Mayfair Witches.*

Winter Horrors

In Iceland, beware Gryla,
the trollish, winter witch
With stalactite tresses
Blue lips and frozen fingers
The mere sight of which
steals breath from lungs
Who enjoys decouring child's meat
And causing Christmas chaos
with her thirteen, mayhem-filled,
Mischievous sons, Yule Lads
And their voracious Yule Cat
With its taste for those unfortunates
Without new holiday clothes

La Befana

Bringer of gifts and bearer of burdens
On Epiphany she comes
With flying broom to tidy households
Personification of the feast

*For La Befana (The Christmas Witch, though she has many names depending on the region) who delivers gifts to good Italian children on Epiphany Eve-5 January. Her ragged clothes and humble headscarf bear soot from chimneys.

Red Woman

Ruthless ruby

Child killer

Calling curses

For kingdom

For sword throne

*Melisandre, the Red Witch or Red Woman (*A Song of Ice and Fire*, George RR Martin) (portrayed by Carice van Houten) shadow demons, blood magic, murders little girls...

Gracious Generations

Mothers and their daughters
A dance through time
Thrown together and torn apart
The essence from the start
Of magical women who like wine
Slip seasons ino starshine

**A Secret History of Witches* by Louisa Morgan, 2017

Slut Salon

To belong or be true to one's own magical art
To conform or create with scathing dark wit
No pastels and pumps, no glittery gloss
No airy voices calling one another "Bunny"
Just night, a dark earth, to dig through forever

*With admiration for Mona Awad's unusual and amusing novel, *Bunny*, 2019

My Favorites from the Wizarding World

Bellatrix the bold
With midnight tangles
Pure blood and dark marked
Insanely wild and wicked

Molly who says,
"Not my daughter!"
Whose greatest fear
Is the death of those
She loves most
Welcoming mother
To more than her blood

Delores Ministry lover
Dressed in head to pinkies
In kittens, teacups, and spite
Topped with prejudice
More hated than even
He Who Shall Not Be Named

Our own Hermione
Fierce friend and loyal student
Legal research as well as school
Concerned with Elfish Welfare
Founder of the D.A.
Smartest of her class

*Though this mentions but my favorite four, this is for all the witches from J.K. Rowling's *Harry Potter* series

Boss Fight

Winged and screeching
Dungeon deep
She lures heroes
Into her keep
Sickle slashing
Shadow fears
Chains do damage
She reappears

*Witch of Hemwick from *Bloodborn* game

Lighthouse

Sometimes we reap what we sow
As most good witches know
On cursed land was built
A time-twisting lighthouse
Where errors its light will show

* *The Lighthouse Witches* by C. J. Cooke, 2021

Wayward

A home for unwed mothers-to-be
To convalesce until delivery
A librarian with ulterior motives
Magic within these women lives
Witches up in the trees
Generations they'll see

*Grady Hendrix's *Witchcraft for Wayward Girls*, 2025

Dahl-ish Witches

As told by Grandma, witches in this world
Are demons with square feet and bald heads,
So they wear wigs as a disguise
They hide their claws by donning gloves
And their eyes can change colors
And since these demons hate children
We must always be on guard
English witches are the most vicious
But all witches turn children into
Loathsome creatures like mice
So their parents and other adults
Will kill them by mistake
So children must always be on guard
Noting if a woman looks like she
Smells something terrible when
Around children, she might be a witch
Ready to transform a child

*Roald Dahl's novel *Witches* presents a stylized vision of almost demonic creatures.

Can't Do A Little

In a quest for a magic flute
Lure a boy with a fancy boat
transform and capture is the aim
others interfere with the game
On Living Island not PC
With psychedelic imagery

*In dubious honor of Witchiepoo with the wicked cackle from the wacky 1969-1970 *H.R. Pufnstuf,* television show.

“False Repressed Memories”

In the beginning, a ritual brings murder
In the woods, wild things occur
In the investigation, frogs fall with rain
In the school, dissection goes wrong
In an interrogation, horror, heartbreak
In the meeting, teachers turn on each other
In the narrative, snake-like hypnotism
In the action, FBI agents assaulted
In the town, undercover Satanists
In the coverup, suicidal student scapegoat
In the end, witch within and without

*Mrs. Paddock, *The X-Files* season 2 “Die Hand Die Verletzt”
Made me think of the Satanic Panic, with rumors of girls being impregnated at an early age so their babies could be harvested as Satanic sacrifices

Magic Girls

Anime amazing
Akko working hard
Battling against
Inner nature until
She believes
In herself

*Akko Kagari in *Little Witch Academia* is not naturally gifted in witchcraft so has to work harder than other girls.

Burning Beauty

When rage is caged
Within a wronged woman
For far too long
Ghost children gasp
Birds fall mid flight
Graveyard dusts sleep
Allies align and
Flames find tongues

*Gwendolyn Kiste's *Boneset and Feathers*, 2020

Toxic Town

Whispers wind around a neck
Coil through like curses
Introspective innocence
Exploitative relatives
Unprotected in patriarchy
Awakened ancient entity
Protective predator
Embraced supernatural

*Brom's *Slewfoot*, 2021

Eat Your Heart Out

Professional and powerful
A witch in disguise
Out of tales and time
Self-made and prized
A villain who helps
Her story redefined

*Regina Mills in the US television show *Once Upon a Time* (2011-2018) played by Lana Parilla inspired this

Mountain Momma

Sometimes the kindest people
Have had the hardest pasts
And gentleness can come
From agonies that last

When warned against another
Take time to get to know
People behind rumors
Their truth will shine and show

*Inspired by *The Hag Witch of Tripp Creek* by Somer Canon, 2019

Gullah Culture

Take a sprinkling of swamp magic
Some Sahara sand
Three of Grandma's precious breaths
Tears wat'ring the land

Fold in some bitter circumstance
Police brutality
A missing Papa and a death
Siblings' love snappy

Add a pinch of loneliness
Vulnerability
A scary doll luring a child
Spirits none can see

***Embracing Root Magic* by Eden Royce, 2021

Witchery and Suffrage

They were suffering without suffrage
Three sisters reunited in New Salem
With hidden agendas honeycombed
With historic happenings
Where magic is the space between
What you have and what you need.

*Using Alix E. Harrow's novel, *The Once and Future Witches*, 2020, as a muse

Female Friendship

Written by a queen of cozy genre fiction
About a newly-single young woman
Who moves from NYC
To a charming village upstate
With a great apartment-
If you ignore the spiders-
And a beautiful friend
Who may be everything she seems

*In honor of *Cackle*, 2021, by Rachel Harrison

Baking Wisdom

Sometimes one must act bravely
And hope for the impossible,
Eat the witch's offerings
Despite their origins
To ask for help takes courage
To accept help is braver still
With time and understanding
Every crumb can lead the way

*Inspired by *The Gingerbread Queen* by Carrie Anne Noble, 2024

Generational Gem

One in a generation
Far removed from the source
Researches the family curse
Earns historic recourse

*Using *A Witch's Penance* by J. K. Divia, 2025, as inspiration

Patriarchal Pariah

Bethel blamed the witches
For every evil emerged
Instead of looking inward

She was lured into Darkwood
Discovered Bethel's deceived
Mother moved between the trees

*In honor of Alexis Henderson's *The Year of the Witching*, 2021

Control

Seventeen Children
Run into the night
A worthy mystery
Delve into history
For a villain to alight

*Inspired by the 2025 film *Weapons*

Dark-Eyed Ladies

Swirling white and black and red
Unusual aesthetic
Pale as bugs beneath cave rocks
With haunted, Halloween eyes
and caring, magical hearts

*For Tim Burton's witches in his films *Sleepy Hollow*, *Dark Shadows*, *Nightmare Before Christmas*, *Beetlejuice Beetlejuice*, and *Alice*.

Cecy, Sweet Cecy

Invisible Inhabitant
Incorporeal invader
Jumps from body to body
Soars as doves as soft as down
Sings the saddest symphony
Perfumes as apple blossoms
Blown by gentle spring breezes
Plays sad songs with cricket legs
Sips seventeen spring dew drops
When beneath a cherry moon
Spring fever sickened Cecy
Possesses Ann - a human girl
Manipulating feeling
She can be in anything
but all she wants to be in
Is love

*Inspired by Ray Bradbury's 1952 short story, "April Witch."

Puritan Paranoia

Brilliant use of metaphor
A witch hunt in Salem
To represent McCarthyism
In Post-World War America
Unfounded mass hysteria
Neighbor turned on friends
Empower the powerless
To misused and evil ends

*Inspired by the play *The Crucible* by Arthur Miller (1953)

Be They Witch or Be they Fairy (or even then a saint)?

I faced a vexing quandary
About who to include
From our marvelous tales
Of yore

Are these fabulous ladies
Witches with fay power
Or are they better claimed
As fay?

From the Canterbury Tales
By author Geoffrey Chaucer
Comes The Wife of Bath's Tale
That tells

Of a young knight of Arthur's
Who accepts a challenge
To discover what gals
Want most

Just before the conclusion
Of a year and a day
He met a wise woman
Who said

(continued)

Women most want sovereignty
Over men and themselves
Her price was he must marry
Her then

They marry and she asks him
Would he rather she be old
And faithful or young and
Faithless?

From his questing time he'd learned
enough to then defer
And give the choice to her
She smiled

Because he learned the answer
To what women wanted most
She turned herself lovely
And true

Then there is Morgan le Fay
From far-flung Camelot
Half-sister to the king
And witch

With the power to enchant
Trap Merlin in an oak
Mislead the Round Table
And more

She caused Camelot's ending
Yet even in her name
"Le Fay" means the fairy
Or witch

Maleficent the Mighty
Next must be considered
Sleeping Beauty's parents
Dissed her

They forgot to invite her
To the princess's christ'ning
He took great offense then
And cursed

Which caused the Sleeping Beauty
And her royal household
One hundred years slumber
Until

A prince came to the rescue
Fought Maleficent and
woke the sleeping princess with
a kiss

Then there's Leicestershire's Black Annis
With her monstrous blue face
iron claws and sharp teeth
Eating kids

Be she a willful fairy
Or a powerful witch
Our interpretation
Decides

Also in this dilemma
Is the Maid of Orleans
Was Joan of Arc a witch
Or saint?

Be they witch or be they fay
Or even then a saint?
My interpretation
Is both

Modern Witch Trials and Personalities

Spiritualism

A darkened room
candle light flickers
The world of spirits
Knocks to be heard
A medium entranced
Conveys messages
Using a voice theirs
And not their own
Automatic writing
Pendulum swings
A talking board
Spirit photos capture
Visitors from beyond
Ectoplasmic emissions
Often debunked
Seance sessions
Horns astounding
Proclaiming "They're here."

*Spiritualism empowered women, allowing them to take the pivotal roles.
*Spiritualism began in the 1800's.
*As the US Civil War was a catalyst for the upsurge of Spiritualism, WWI provided the spur for this mystical belief in Europe.

Three Sisters

Knocks and rapping
Attention called
A murdered peddler
Spirit not at rest
Three girls together
Speak spirit sessions
Soulful seer seances
Spiritualism stars

*The Fox Sisters, Leah, Margarette, and Katherine, from Hydesville, New York, USA used rapping from spirits to interpret messages from the dead.
*They had a profound influence on the Spiritualist Movement.
*Later in life, two of the sisters refuted their contacts with the "other side."

Biddy Early

Born into humble means
With a wise mother
Who taught the old ways,
Pretty Biddy caught the eye
Of many a man
In Feakle, people came
To ask this wise woman
For healing and charms
Which with love she provided;
She clashed with the church
But remained in good standing
With her community where she
Became something of a
Folk hero and legend.

*Bridget Ellen Connors was born in 1798 and died of natural causes in 1874, predeceased by four husbands. Tourists can view the ruins of her home in Feakle, County Claire, Ireland.

Hint of Hellfire

A smear of hot chili paste across the eyes
To hint of future Hellfire
Hands boiled in oil and swung
From damaged arms above a bonfire
For days until she confessed
Or died or died confessing

*In 1886, the elderly woman, Kunkoo, was accused of inflicting illness on an Indian soldier's wife. These were her tortures before she was murdered for her alleged crimes.
*British authorities implemented bans on witch killing between 1840 and 1860 throughout Eastern India. These bans apparently drove the practices underground, with many enacted as resistance against colonial power.
*To this day, the National Crime Records Bureau reports cases of witch branding.

Hexenwahn (witch mania)

An esoteric and evil Nazi
Obsessed with an imagined ancestor
A paragon of Aryan women
In touch with the Germanic Pagan pulse

*SS officer Heinrich Himmler organized an investigation (Hexenkartothek or the H-Special Order Project) into the witch trials to prove they were a plot by the Catholic church and the Jewish people to rob Germany of its heritage and exterminate Aryan womanhood.
*The gathered information was supposed to be presented in a propaganda book. No book was presented, and researcher Rudolf Levin's Habilitation Thesis was rejected by the Munich University in 1944.
*Himmler, who believed he was descended from a witch, also tried to create his own, Nazi-themed religion involving witchcraft-inspired spectacles incorporating fire, solstices, shadows, witch dances, and drums. He apparently believed witches like those in Grimm's fairy tales were misrepresented, Germanic seeresses who possessed spiritual powers.

Science of the Soul

She blended science and the occult
Psychology and psychic defense
Through esoteric symbolism
Ritual, meditation, and study
Member of the Golden Dawn
Combined cabbalistic teachings
Included Energy manipulation
Taught Magic is the science of the soul
Inspires seekers to this day
Through her written works

*Dion Fortune (born Violet Mary Firth, author, Mystical Christian, and ceremonial magician who made contributions to the craft. Founded the Fraternity of the Inner Light in 1924 - dealt with alternate realities and religious and magical philosophies. Died in 1946)

Medium At Large

Born on Christmas morning
Helen Duncan told fortunes
A medium of some acclaim
She conjured the deceased

She traveled around Britain
Performing seances
Produced ectoplasmic evidence
For grieving families

The London Spiritual Alliance
And others of the times
Tried to disprove her abilities
Still she carried on

She called upon the spirit
Of a sailor who had died
On the HMS Barham
Which drew Naval attention

None but the sailors' families
Knew of the sunken ship
So how she knew of its fate
Was reason for concern

The World War Two War Office
Declared her a security risk
And under an old Witchcraft Act
Made her serve prison time

*Helen Duncan was the last woman convicted and imprisoned under Great Britain's Witchcraft Act of 1735. She was a psychic medium who allegedly talked to the spirit of a sailor who died on the HMS Barham. The problem arose because the War Office hadn't released the information of the sinking of the ship! They decided if she could Predict naval attacks, she was a security risk. She was arrested for fraudulent witchcraft in 1944 and served 9 months of prison time. She died in 1956.

Alarming Alabama

Gadsden, Alabama boomed
Despite the Great Depression
But the cost, oh the cost!

A lovely, ageless woman
Walked her gold-collared hound
Along the shady pathways
In the surrounding woods

To stay young and vibrant
A witch must gather ingredients
But the cost, oh the cost!

The elders of Gadsden
Knew to woodland dangers
But turned a blind eye
To secure prosperity

First a few, and then many
Of the town's youngest members
Became the cost, oh the cost!

She twisted backward, screeching
As she claimed unsuspecting children
To become spell ingredients
Needed for youth and wealth

A concerned group of parents
Murdered her to end child murders
Oh, the cost, oh the cost!

To this day, no plants grow
On the burned-out foundation
Of the house of the wicked witch
Who bought youth with offered wealth

To Know Ved'ma

Fusing Village wisdom
With rituals and prayers
Cleansing and spellcasting
Candle burning and Tarot
Uniting eras and countries
Working, collaborating
Connecting with the past
To merge the present
For all the future times

*Practicing modern Witchcraft is on the rise in Russia since the fall of the Soviet Union.
*According to Health Ministry data from 2017, nearly 1 million people in Russia earn a living through witchcraft-related skills such as folk healing, psychic mediumship, and prognostication.
*Not everyone in Russia embraces witchcraft's return. There were reports of persecution of accused witches in Chechnya in 2020, where Muslims are the majority. In 1997, two Russian farmers reportedly assaulted a woman and injured five family members, believing they had used witchcraft against them.

Like Avenging Ninjas

Cloaked in darkness,
Masked assailants
Fell upon their victims-
Disembowelling
Beheading-
Before disappearing
Unmolested vigilantes
Into cloaking darkness

*The collapse of the Suharto Era in Indonesia in 1998 was accompanied by vigilante witch hunts, resulting in approximately 400 killings in the following years.

Tanzania

Another hot, dry day
A day like many others
When a soul-dark fire
Licked the heat-seared sky
Cracked the craven heart
Ruined families
With accusatory smiles
From a witchfinder
A swath of charred land
Marks the victims' unrest

*Tanzanian Witch Trials 1960-2000, an estimated tens of thousands of people were murdered due to accusation of witchcraft, often through village tribunals.
*During the Tanzanian Witch Hunts in 2005-2011, more than 3,000 ppl believed to be witches were lynched.
*In 2016, at least 400 women were killed in Tanzania as witches

Green Boys Marching

Drums announce their coming

Vigilante Green Boys on the march

And their informant shamans

Dressed in blood red tunics

Cowry charms clanging

Mirrors reflecting coming crime

*Under orders from the dictator Yahya Jammeh, Gambian government sponsored witch hunts led to abductions, beatings, rape, poisoning, forced confessions, and death
*The UN is investigating the long-term effects and possibilities for reconciliation
(Popoviciu, Andrei, “Thousands of Gambians Were Accused of Witchcraft and Tortured. Can Theri Country Make Them Whole?” *New Line Magazine* Online, 18 August, 2023.)
(Amnesty.Org, “The Gambia: Hundreds Accused of Witchcraft and Poisoned in Government Campaign,” 18 March, 2009.)

Witchcraft Murder in Great Britain

Valentines Day
A time for happy hearts
Found a heart burst
A man of seventy
A bloody cross
carved into his chest
Battered with a wooden stick
Pinned to the ground
With his own pitchfork
Through his neck

On Ash Wednesday
To restore fertility
Replenish the earth
In an unfruitful time
To counter a curse
Made by the man
Said to tie a toy plow
To a toad and set it free
Causing blighted lands
And poor harvest

*On 14 February, 1945, which was both St. Valentine's Day and Ash Wednesday, Meon Hill Hedgecutter, Charles Walton was murdered.
*In September, 1875, a woman named Ann Tennant was murdered the same way in a nearby village. Her murderer confessed that he killed her to rid the area of her witchcraft. The memory of Ann's Murder brought up suspicions of witchcraft as a motivation for Charles Walton's murder.
*Celebrated Egyptologist, ninety-year-old Margaret Murray assisted police and the Yard with a witchcraft theory.

Bottle Blonde

Dingy blonde roles and nudity
Playmate of the month
Queen of the wardrobe malfunction
"Drive-in Marilyn"
Rendezvous with the Satanic
Brought a fiery end

*Jayne Mansfield is said to have participated in Anton LeVey's Satanic services, and when she left the practice, some theorize her automobile accident was orchestrated by LeVey and his group. LeVey's daughter, however, said the curse that their group leveled did not target 34-year-old Jayne but her lover, Samuel S. Brody who was in the car when the gruesome 1967 car accident took place.

Corpse-Carrying

Paraded through a village

A body recently dead

Reeking of rot and ruin

Rigor Mortis in the limbs

Points out their lethal culprit

The witch who caused their end

*In much of Ghana, witch hunting primarily targets elderly women.
More than 500 people resided in witch camps when Amnesty International visited in April, 2024.
*Some refugee camps for women accused of witchcraft in Ghana were established in the early 20th century and still operational today.
* "The government should establish a long-term national awareness campaign challenging cultural and social practices that discriminate against women and old people." Genevieve Partington, Country Director of Amnesty International Ghana, 2025.
*Witch hunts are also common practices in Kenya, Nigeria, Tanzania, and Zambia.

Nepali Identification

Unfortunate women with
Facial hair or baldness
Stooped posture
Infertility,
Reddened or yellowed eyes
Who talk to themselves
Or are difficult and
Untraditional
Clearly must be witches,
Or so it's said in Nepal

The accused are
stripped naked
Faces blackened with soot
Or battery powder
Shaved bald
(self-fulfilling)
With a necklace of shoes
Hung round her neck
Fed excrement
Palms burned
And made to inhale
Burning chillies

*Many of the accused are Nepali widows who are accused of murdering their own husbands. This prevents the accused from inheriting property, since witches are not allowed to own land.
*Male magic men assist in the proceedings, lending their 'authority,' though the violence is often enacted by the accused's own community.
*INSEC reported 52 incidents against women in 2012, 69 in 2013, and 89 in 2014.
*A shelter was set up in Kathmandu for victims of the witch hunts.
*The Anti-Witchcraft Act of 2014 was enacted to curb witch hunting.
*The Women's Rehabilitation Center and The Women's Foundation of Nepal work to regain women's rights.
*Federici, Silvia, "Women, Witch-Hunting, and Enclosures in Africa Today," Social Geschichte Online, 2010.

Burley Village, Witches Village

Burley Village, Witches Village
Quaint and full of charm
With thatched-roofed cottages
Many magical shoppes
(Including Coven of Witches
Which was named by
"Britain's Most Famous Witch"
Sybil Leek)
Proud producers of
Spellbinding ciders and wines
Haunted by phantoms
Astral, ancestral visitors
Wafting with fogs
And sage breezes
Alongside friendly ponies
And proud, prancing pigs
Strolling the ambling High Street
Or the haunting horsemen
Clip clopping down Lane and Lawn

Past the Center for Pagan Studies
(Founded by Gerald Brosseau Gardener
"The Father of Modern Witchcraft")
fairy-ringed by New Forest
Wild, wonderful woodlands
Dense, historic witnesses
Imbued with the mystic
From years of practice
Home to an ancient dragon
Or so the legends say

*Burley Village resident and author Sybil Leek was named by the BBC as the "Most Famous Witch in Britain" in the 1950's. Her outspoken charisma and audacious, cloak-wearing, bird bringing appearance garnered oodles of attention domestically and internationally. Unfortunately, she passed away in 1982.

Descendents

Good women, some would say
Godly, honest, strong
Though some had their own debts needed to pay
Difficult women, some assert
Loud, acerbic, blunt
Their opinions they never failed to blurt
Quiet women, "odd men out"
Different, dangerous, dark
Yet their descendents today proudly shout
These women, one and all
Accused of witches' craft
Their descendents want their memories to stand
tall

*Incorporated on 6 August, 1986, the Associated Daughters of Early American Witches searches for and preserves the names of those accused of witchcraft in that portion of Colonial America which became the United States of America.

Fifty

Fifty people accused

Fifty called witches

Fifty people died

In two highlands

In one year alone-

2008-

In Papua New Guinea

*Witchcraft was declared an official crime in Papua New Guinea from 1971-2013.

India Injustice

"You're not human,"
The merchants scream,
As they refuse
To accept her
Ration card

Children of accused
Are targeted
The families left
Destitute
Ostracized

"No mercy," they say
As they strike, spit
Throw garbage, shit
At the accused
And seize property

The lucky escape
With only their lives
And find a group
Of other women
Likewise accused

*In India, from 2005 to mid 2015, 2000 women were named as witches.
*Some were "Forced to drink human waste, because after drinking human waste, a witch is cured."
*A witch is not allowed to own property, so it's suspected many accusations are attempts to steal property from vulnerable women, especially widows. These women are exiled.
*A group of accused "witches" bound together to form an organization called Anandi to help other unfortunate women in the same situation.
*Daain law introduced in Bihar condemning witchcraft resulted in property seizure, beatings, and other atrocities.
*Although some local areas prohibit the practice, at the time of this writing there's no national legislation to prevent witch hunts.
*Chapra, 1849, Eullai was accused, her property was seized, she was tortured, and killed.
*21 Districts in Assam reportedly participate in witch hunts since 2014.
*Private organizations like the Centre for Social Justice and Mission Birubala (started by Birrubala Rabha) fight for the rights and assets of women and marginalized people attacked in witch hunts.
*In 2021, the Indian Government enacted the Assam Witch Hunting Act which is said to be India's toughest anti-witch hunting legislation to date.
*Information obtained from the NCRB, 2024, New York Times, 2016, Numerous newscasts from Vice Asia and DW.

"Get learned, not burned"

From impoverished Roma groups
Witchcraft wriggles roots
Preserving folk traditions
In ancestral grounds

*A Romanian witch school opened outside of Bucharest in 2024. Overseen by one of Europe's most powerful witches - Mahaelia.
*Roma people in 2011 protested taxes leveled against witches. Other religious organizations are not taxed there.

At Times and Places

Danger descends on a woman who
Calls upon inner reserves
Speaks aloud dangerous thoughts
In the wrong area
Or to an antagonistic audience

*Amina Bint Abdul Halim Nassar was beheaded for allegedly practicing witchcraft in Saudi Arabia in 2011. An Anti-witchcraft Unit was set up in Saudi Arabia in 2009.

Bad Blood in San Antonio

A coven of four in Texas
Caught a woman to be defiled
Held her captive and drugged her
Cut her hair and took her blood
She was rescued by the sheriff
Before the final sacrifice

*2015, USA

Wicked Women

Some take the role of wicked witch
And embrace its evil schemes
Like Angela who made a sacrifice
Of Joel Leyva in New Mexico
Or Diana in Ventura, California
Who killed a wife as a gift for her lover
Cara and Dale took their role-play too far
She a witch, he her demon lover
Also in Ventura, California - something in the sand?
Cherrylle Dell used her skills to calm her husband
To trick him into drinking antifreeze in wine
And seduced a teen into murdering her accuser
Heather Miller had a fellow witch who reported to police
About Heather's attempts to murder her husband
Mari met her end when her daughter believed
Her witchy ways had resulted in a possession

*These modern women took their calling to be wicked seriously. Angela Sanford murdered Joel Leyva in 2010 using a ceremonial knife. Diana Haun, another self-professed witch, killed her lover Michael Dally's wife as a sacrificial gift to celebrate his birthday in 1996. Carol Williams-Covert and Dale Farquhar Larry Roger Fisk in 2009 as a way of acting out a play, or as a sacrifice to Satan, or to start a killing spree. Cherrylle Dell murdered her husband, Scott, in 1995. Her teen conquest burned Nancy Fillmore in 1997 after she testified against Cherrylle. Heather Miller's neighbor, fellow witch, and lover, Mindi, wore a police wire to gather information about her plans to kill Kevin, Heather's husband in 2000. Mari Gilbert, an active participant in the occult since her teen years, was murdered by her daughter, Sarra, in Ellenville, New York in 2016.

Confidence

She relied on self-confidence
To woo her victims then
She relied on their confidence
In her abilities to help them
She used info got in confidence
To provide her services
Partners walked with confidence
To deposit more than sixty K
They relied on the confidence
Of their victim's embarrassment
To keep them safe from prosecution.

*In October, 2018 Dorie Medina Stevenson (age 32 from Milton, Ontario) & a week later, Samatha Stevenson (Just like Bewitched?) were charged under Criminal Code Section 365 which made it illegal in Canada to fraudulently pretend to exercise or to use any kind of witchcraft, sorcery, enchantment, or conjuration. They apparently used Dorie's company, Milton Psychic, to defraud more than $60,000 from a customer.
* 5 other people were charged under this section of the law since the turn of the century before it was repealed at the end of 2018.

Accused in Church

Sleeper cell in service
Called out from the pulpit
By a brimstone-bashing pastor
Who tells of talks with demons
Who expose the wily witches
The sleeper cell in service

*In Tennessee, Pastor Greg Locke of Global Vision Bible Church in early 2022 accused six of his parishioners of being witches. He is also known for book burnings and asserting Covid-19 was a fake pandemic. He doubled down on his witchcraft beliefs in December, 2022 by tweeting on X that his family was threatened by witchcraft. (Bickerton, James, Newsweek Online, December 20, 2022)

For the Win

La Brujineta
Cabala convened
Thirty thousand strong
With witchy wishes
Energy enhanced
Football enthused
Argentina armed

*A group of energy workers and spiritual witches convened online and in person to heal and protect the players of their Argentina football team during the World Cup in 2023. Like most of South America, Argentina has a long and varied history of spiritual practices.

Grecian Dilemma

A newly-minted citizen of Greece
Applied for her ID Card
And stalled at a question:
"Declare religion"
Hers absent from the list
What to do when a witch
In modern-day Greece?

*As of 2024, Hellenism or other pagan belief systems are not accepted as religions in Greece. (Ironic, since Hellenism is a modern adaptation of spiritual practices reviving those from Ancient Greece.)

Brujería y Más

Feminist manifestation
Proud proclamations ring out
Down with the patriarchy
power to the witch

Many cultures bring influence
Spiritualism sings slow
Ancestors swim through the blood
Supernatural

*Latin American witchcraft blends Regional
Indigenous, Catholic, African, and European beliefs.

New Old Religion

Wiccan worship with witchy, wildlife wiles
Pagan practitioners progressing
Polytheistic reconstruction beguiles
German Heathenry with Norse connection
Neo-Druidry as in the ancient isles
The Satanic Temple does as they wilt
Pantheistic province, Animistic styles
Christopaganism combines cultures
Combined with what Hebrews called gentiles
Many modes of worship personally honed
Redefining religious lifestyles

*As many as three million people in the United States of America today identify as witches.
*Hundreds to thousands of on-line resources are devoted to sharing information and concerns about witchcraft.

Witch of King's Cross

Pan performer
Sensual sex
Willowy influencer

Hypnotiser
Liberal
Entrancing magic user

*Although she died in 1979, Rosaleen Norton (2 October, 1917-5 December, 1979) remains a key influence in Australia's pagan communities.

Divine Queen

Born on history-rich soil
Of the fabled West Country
While golden rays of dawn
Danced to your bird-sweet songs
Read from the mystic's cards
You put your pen to use
With tales of green goddess
And her hidden horned king
Indoctrinated youth
Widespread coven conclaves
Verbal olde religions

*Rhiannon Ryall, resident of Perth, authored many books, some controversial.

Cooperative Crafts

Raised with housebound spirits
Whispering grave secrets
Cold winds carried soul-sure
Bowing to Faerie courts
Flickering finery
Trooping floral perfume
Intuition as guide
winning wisdom from stars

*Julia Phillips's Pagan Alliance in Australia fosters ties between Australian and New Zealand neopagan groups.

Cultural Quandary

Hidden messages in music
Damnation from D&D
Preschools in peril
Virgin violations
Infant sacrifice
Animals abused
cannibalism
Widespread accusation
Arrests, ruination
Leading interviews
False repressed memories
No evidence ever produced

*The Satanic Panic of the 1980's and 1990's overtook the media and imaginations of the USA, resulting in over 12,000 unsubstantiated cases of Satanic ritual abuse. Many people spent time in jail as a result.
*Canadian book Michelle Remembers written by psychologist Lawrence Pazder detailed ritualistic child abuse and Satanism and was used almost as a template for devastating investigations.

Q

It started as a whisper
An anonymous report
Connected and organized
Evil-doing Satanists
High in Hollywood
Placed in Politics
Child Trafficking
Ritual Sacrifice
To further Agendas

*QAnon started in 2016 and revived the idea of the Satanic Underground being fought by far right political activists.
*There's a pervasive theory that the media and celebrities in particular use witchcraft to further themselves.

Hanover, Hanover, Hanover

In Pennsylvania lives a law
Suppressing tarot reading
Or other “witchy ways”
“For gain or lucre”

*After a 2023 near-arrest in Hanover, Pennsylvania, Beck Ravenswood Lawrence, who owns and operates The Serpent’s Key, a “witch shoppe and sanctuary,” is fighting against the 1861 Pennsylvania law on the basis of religious freedom.

Ambition

In covens or alone
They claim their magic powers
Entertain the masses
Bewitch them for long hours

*Vampira actress Nalia Nurmi, Singers Lady Gaga, Jennifer Lopez, Beyonce, Arianna Grande, and artist Marina Abramovich, have been accused of practicing witchcraft. To date, none of these ladies has claimed the title themselves.

Young and Magical

She launched a quest
"Find ingredients online"
Use the magic words
"Bigger than your own vibrations"
At the ridding time
When a waning crescent moon
Hangs low in the sky
At midnight magic's made

*Lana Del Rey invited fans and left-leaning practicing witches and occultists to participate in a ritual to keep Donald Trump from office in 2017. (DiMeglio, Mary J., "Lana Del Rey Reveals She Used Witchcraft Against Trump," Billboard Online, 24 July, 2017.)
*Right-leaning Witches for Trump performed counter ceremonies.

Pregame Rituals

She erected an altar
Predicted win or lose
Gave her man mantras
Handed him healing stones
And prayed for his protection
On the field and in the home
*Supermodel Gisselle Bundchen married football player Tom Brady in 2009. In an interview, he said she asserted, “You’re lucky you married a witch.” The couple divorced in 2022.

*In a March, 2023 interview with *Vanity Fair*, she said, “If you want to call me a witch because I love astrology, I love crystals, I pray, I believe in the power of nature, then go ahead.”

Pan Pipes

In the City of Angels
A spiritual store
Saved from closing
By a witchy actress
Revived by another

*Although she doesn't claim to be a witch, Fairuza Balk, the actress of Nancy in 1996's *The Craft*, bought the occult bookstore PanPipes in 2001 in gratitude for the guidance from the purveyors while she was on set and to prevent it from being made into a restaurant.

*Gabrielle Anwar, actress from *Once Upon a Time* and *Scent of a Woman*, bought it from Fairuza.

Hunter's Moon Manifested

Gathered together
Beneath a bright, full moon
Lavender and magic
Their power proven

*Paris Jackson wrote about starting a coven with some spiritual friends on Instagram, October, 2021.

Surrounded by Trees and Song

The voice of a songbird
A soul of the earth
Connected to angels
Seeing spirits and rebirth

*Vanessa Anne Hudgens is an actress and singer who announced herself as a witch many times, including in a witchcraft documentary and a Nylon interview, 2023.

Between Healing and Heresy

Be it idolatry or necromancy
(communing with the dead)
Forbidden to practice
As it worships other gods
Or produces something
Other than illusion
Unless miraculous
Like Moses' displays
Or prophetic proclamation
Or even a gollum
Mysticism of Kabbalah

*Hebrew scholars debate the differences between witchcraft and the miraculous.

Seized

Against Allah
Antagonistic
Folk remedies
Misogynistic

It matters not
Sympathetic magic
All perceived as
Intended to harm

*The Committee for the Promotion of Virtue and the Prevention of Vice established an anti-witchcraft unit in Saudi Arabia in 2009 which included at hotline for reporting suspected witches
*June, 2015, The Islamic State beheaded two women in Syria for witchcraft (source: Syrian Observatory for Human Rights)

Media controlled

In 91 BC, during the reign of Emperor Wu of Han,
Members of the Imperial Court and Shamans
Carried out a witch hunt.
These days Gong Tau is when someone's suspected
Of being attacked by black magic and poison,
But magic can help with other things.

*China has laws against Witchcraft and any religion outside of the five recognized religions.
*In July, 2024, an "internet celebrity" who practiced witchcraft online was prosecuted under China's penal code against "cults."

Tartan

Woven with integrity
Wrapping wrongs with wool
History threaded through
The Blackness of heartache
Made ashen with women
Reduced to embers after
Bound by
Red tape and paler views
To serve as a lasting
Pardon, apology, memorial

*To obtain a piece of Scottish, witchy-craze history, contact Prickly Thistle's
Claire Mitchell and Zoe Venditozzi for the Witches of Scotland tartan

Witches of Scotland Campaign

Zoe and Claire
Fight for pardons
For all those killed
As witches
Resistance in remembrance

E.J.J. - The Last Salem Witch

Teacher Carrie LaPierre
And two devoted years
of classroom Civics students
Introduced legislation
to exonerate
Elizabeth Johnson, Jr.,
The only Salem "witch"
whose good name
Remained uncleared

* *The Last Witch* Film tells the story of this incredible journey, proving "It's never too late for justice."

Even Today

The headline screams of attacks and death
Though the Ghanaian parliament passed a bill
Which made it a criminal offense
to even name someone as a witch -
That bill has yet to be made a law

Sadly, the threats, attacks, and death
Often start within the family or community
After tragedy, sickness, or death -
Often targeting the least protected

Older women enduring poverty
or poor health or disabilities
Or non-conforming, free-thinking women -
Banishment to priest-run camps or death

"Children of witchcraft" are beaten
Branded as unclean witches
And abandoned in the -
Democratic Republic of Congo

Anti-albinism protections are not in place
With over 150 people abducted and never
Seen in their Malawi, Africa homes again alive -
Body parts used for spellcraft or killed for difference

Babies born feet first, face up in
The Republic of Benin
Are believed to be witches -
Abandoned, abused, and assassinated

*Amnesty International released a report on the human rights abuses in Ghana in April, 2025. As a result of these abuses, organizations such as the Nigerian-based non-profit Advocacy for Alleged Witches and the Coalition Against Witchcraft Accusations.

*The problem is not restricted to Ghana, either. Just last year, in 2024, Eight women accused of using witchcraft to cause the death of two ailing boys in Guinea Bissau were forced to drink poison and died. In the Congo, two elderly women were publicly stoned and their bodies burned, and in Angola, about 50 people were forced to drink an herbal concoction to prove they were not magic users. The UN and Christian Missionaries International are trying to set up safe orphanages, shelters, and homes for those targeted as witches in Africa.

*Human Rights Watch has since 2009 repeatedly asked for a cessation of state-sanctioned, loosely defined witch hunts in Saudi Arabia. Those convicted for using witchcraft are often executed.

*Although Tribal and Balit women are the most vulnerable, women in modern India are in danger of being accused of and punished for witchcraft. According to India's National Crime Bureau, more than 2,500 people (98% women) were killed as witches between 2000 and 2016.

*In parts of India and nepal between 2000-2012 alone, at least 2,100 lynchings and murders of accused witches were reported by The Times of India (March and October, 2008), Sky News (14 August, 2015), Asian Journal of Women's Studies 22 (2 January, 2016), The Economist (19 October, 2017),

*A rock called "Boksimara" which means "witch killer stone" is where accused women in Terhathum were (and are) hanged for practicing witchcraft.

*This is far from an exhaustive look at modern witch hunts and personalities, but it's important to know how pervasive the very real dangers of mob mentality and "othering" people continues to be. When I talked with friends about this project, few knew of the atrocities that continue to this day.

Ending Thoughts

The old-world, religious idea of a witch was one who spat on God, said prayers backward, and literally kissed the devil's behind. In European-influenced society, it pointed to a desecration of all the churches held as holy. It purposely misused the symbols and adulterated innocence and goodness.

If I am understanding it correctly, this perspective would be more in line with Satanism, though there is an active church of Satan in America today, and I am not certain the participants call themselves Satanists, Occultists, or Witches.

The modern pagan has a different interpretation of witchcraft. There are practitioners of Wicca, Druids, NeoPagans, independent practitioners, mountain magic users, Pow Wowers, Conjure Women, and New Age Practitioners, to name but a few, and those few more Euro-centric only because of my limited knowledge. (I hope to learn more about witchcraft in other cultures as I continue to study. Those I did include were for inclusion and appreciation, not appropriation.)

As with any person in any religion or belief system, there are those who endeavor to do "good" and those who are not concerned with morality. Unlike Glenda when she meets Dorothy, though, one can't be distinguished as one or the other by looks, only by actions. (And there's much to say for all being a bit of both.) There's a wealth of information available for those interested.

However, the idea of a witch as a symbol of feminine power, a way to stand against the problems of toxic patriarchy, intrigues me. Be she a wild woman in a swamp, a creature of fairy tale horror, or the lady at the board meeting with a superbly fitted suit, witches remain radical creatives, ungovernable nonconformists. They're cunning, strong willed, and wise, not to mention sexy. They challenge the status quo. They embrace their own potential and power.

It is interesting how the interpretation of the witch has changed through time. However, they've always been divisive and a bit of a contradiction. In antiquity, witches were terrifying, necromantic baby-snatchers to be avoided, or they were revered, respected, and protected seers and healers. They were both at the same time. Women of every walk of life have been accused of witchcraft, but the motivation for the accusations often differ with social standing. In Puritan times, the witch was touted as a pathetic, weak creature granted powers by the devil who subjugated her in exchange for his gifts. These days, the witch remains a Halloween staple, and she is more often interpreted by the American media as a sexy, self-possessed, empowered, and powerful woman.

I wish I could represent every person accused of, and murdered because of, witchcraft, but there are simply too many to be contained in this volume -

Literally thousands in the past and present. However, this book is an acknowledgement of their experiences and lives, with a bit of whimsy included in the middle. If you know other stories and wish to share, I would love to hear from you! Feel free to contact me.

And as I expressed at the beginning of this collection, there are many amazing male witches, but I believe these magical women deserved a book of their own. Besides, I hope to explore masculine witchcraft another time with an upcoming project.

Blessed Be

Do No Harm

The power of three

One with nature

God Bless!

Further Reading

Throughout this collection, I mention some amazing works of witchy-inspired art. Please check them out! I think you'll be as enchanted as I was when first I discovered them.

For some more scholarly sources, these are helpful:

White Thomas, *Witches of Pennsylvania*, The History Press, 2013.

White, Thomas, *The Witch of the Monongahela*, The History Press, 2020.

Henderson, Lizanne, *Witchcraft and Folk Belief in the Age of Enlightenment: Scotland 1670-1740*, Palgrave McMillan, 2017.

Macdonald, S., "In Search of the Devil in Fife Witchcraft Cases, 1560-1705," *The Scottish Witch-Hunt in Context*, Manchester University Press.

Upham, Charles, *Salem Witchcraft*, Frederick Ungar Publishing, 1980.

Hill, Frances, *The Salem Witch Trials Reader*, De Capo Press, 1974.

Baker, Emerson W., *A Storm of Witchcraft: The Salem Trials and the American Experience* Oxford University Press, 2015.

Karlson, Carol F., *The Devil in the Shape of a Woman: Witchcraft in Colonial New England*, W.W. Norton, New York, 1998.

Rosenthal, Bernard, *Salem Story: Reading the Witch Trials of 1692*, Cambridge U. Press, Cambridge, 1993.

Burns, Willam E., *Witch Hunts in Europe and America: An Encyclopedia*, Greenwood Press, 2003.

Gibson, Marion, Witchcraft: *A History in 13 Trials*, Scribner, 2024.

Roach, Marilynn K., *Six Women of Salem: The Untold Story*, MJF Books, 2013.

Durrant, Jonathan Bryan, *Witchcraft, Gender, and Society in Early Modern Germany*, Brill, 2007.

Machielsen, Jan, *The Basque Witch Hunt: A Secret History*, Bloomsbury Academic Press, 2024.

Shachat, Emma, “The Antisemitic History of Witches,” HeyAlma.com, October, 2020.

“German Beer Brewing Witches? The Dark History of Women Brewers,” GermanGirlinAmerica.com,

*Wood, Jay Maxwell, *Witchcraft and Superstitious Record*

*Gregerson, John, *Witchcraft and Second Sight in the Highlands and Islands of Scotland*

Louise Yeoman, “The Woman Who Became a Witch Pricker,” *BBC News Scotland Online*, 18 November, 2012.

Kroll, David, “The Origin of Witches Riding Broomsticks: Drugs from Nature,” *Forbes Magazine*, 31 October, 2017.

Mann, John, *Murder, Magic, and Medicine*, Oxford University Press, 1992.

Sneddon, Andrew, *Possessed by the Devil: The Real History of the Islandmagee Witches and Ireland's Only Mass Witchcraft Trial*, History Press, 2013.

Gaskill, Malcolm, *The Ruin of All Witches: Life and Death in the New World*, Random House, November, 2022.

"Puritan's Witch Trial Notebook from Tatton Park Online," *BBC News England Online*, 3 March, 2011.

Foster, Helen, "Tales of the Burley Witches," Differentville.com, 2025.

Sanderson, Sertan, "Witch Hunts: A Global Problem in the 21st Century, *DW Online*, 2025.

"Witchcraft Accusations Putting Hundreds at Risk of 'Physical Attacks or Even Death' in Ghana, Amnesty Says," *CBS News*, April, 2025.

W Magazine, "Six Celebrities Who Have Been Accused of Witchcraft," Munzenreider, Kyle, October, 2018.

Rojas, Rochelle E., *Bad Christians and Hanging Toads: Witch Trials in Early Modern Spain*, 1525-1675, Duke University Press (Dept. of History - doctoral dissertation), 2016.

Fua, Amber, Ranker, "12 Real Crimes Involving Modern-Day Witches and Witchcraft," 2020. https://www.ranker.com/list/crimes-committed-by-modern-witches/amber-fua

Garc, Beatriz A., "Against Terrorist Witchcraft!" *Al Dia*, 29 May, 2020.

Romero Nunez, Fernando, *Buenos Aires Herald*, "How 30,000 Witches Helped Argentina Win the World Cup," 25 December, 2023.

~

Some court records are available on Project Gutenberg and through university and museum libraries and collections

~

Also, the Scottish Tartan Project:
https://instagram.com/witches.of.scotland

Rebecca Nurse Homestead, Danvers, Massachusetts

Justice for Witches project (English lobbying to grant posthumous pardons for "witches") led by Charlotte Meredith

Gresham College "Witchcraft Problem Today" lecture online (YouTube)

"Accused of Witchcraft in New York" by S.R. Ferrara (Feb, 2023 release) Online Talk hosted by the Chapman Museum on 11 October, 2023

Possible Playlist

It can be (and has been) argued that the music industry owes much to witches and the occult. I don't necessarily mean in the literal sense like Robert Johnson, the blues guy who sold his soul at the crossroads.... However, there is reportedly more than a bit of that, too. (I'm looking at you, Jimmy Page.) Rumors of backmasking secret messages into rock songs fed into the Satanic Panic of the 1980's. Many artists embraced this non-conformist imagery to boost sales. Some apparently used their platform to proselytize their beliefs.

There's no way I'll remember all of the possible inclusions on this list. Not only is my memory not that great, but there's such a wide world of music to explore, and I'm sure I've missed many amazing musical interpretations of the theme. However, I've included different genres and styles of music to explore.

If you have any you'd like to see added, I'd love to hear your suggestions! Send them to me in a note on my website: https://www.KerryEBBlack.com or my blog Allusionary Assembly at www.kerrylizblack.wordpress.com

Some Songs for Witchy Moods

Dream of a Witches' Sabbath (Hector Berlioz, 1827),
Witchcraft (Frank Sinatra, 1957),
That Old Black Magic (Ella Fitzgerald, 1961),
The Witch (The Sonics, 1965),
Do You Believe in Magic (The Lovin' Spoonful, 1967),
Strange Brew (Cream, 1967),
Wicked Annabella (The Kinks, 1968),
My Girlfriend is a Witch (October Country, 1968),
Curse of the Witches (Strawberry Alarm Clock, 1968),
Put a Spell on You (Screaming Jay Hawkins, 1956, Nina Simone, 1957, Creedence Clearwater Revival, 1968),
Black Magic Woman (Santana, 1968),
Season of the Witch (Donovan, Karen Elson, 2011, and Lana Del Rey, 2021), "Pick Up Every Stitch"
Crimson Witch (The Moving Sidewalks, 1969),
Bad Moon Rising (Creedence Clearwater Revival, 1969),
The Witch (The Rattles, 1970),
Spill the Wine (Eric Burdon & War, 1970),
Witch's Promise (Jethro Tull, 1970),
The Witch Queen of New Orleans, (Redbone, 1971),
Superstition (Stevie Wonder, 1972),
Witchy Woman (The Eagles, 1972),
Rhiannon (Fleetwood Mac, 1972),
Wild Witch Lady (Donovan 1973),
Marie Laveau (Bobby Bare, 1973),
Dark Lady (Cher, 1974),
Devil Woman (Cliff Richard, 1976),
The Mummers' Dance (Loreena McKennitt, 1977),
Witches' Song (Marianne Faithful, 1979),
Sisters of the Moon (Fleetwood Mac, 1979),

Witch Hunt (Rush, 1981), "The night is black, without a moon, the air is thick and still, vigilantes gather on the lonely torchlit hill"
Spellbound (Siouxsie and the Banshees, 1981, "Following the footsteps of a rag doll dance, we are entranced, spellbound..."),
Abracadabra (Steve Miller Band, 1982),
Eye in the Sky (Alan Parsons Project, 1982),
You Can Do Magic (America, 1982),
Don't Burn the Witch (Venom, 1982),
Black Magic (Slayer, 1983),
Wrapped Around Your Finger (The Police, 1983, "I have only come here seeking knowledge. Things they would not teach me of in college..."),
Come to the Sabbath (Mercyful Fate, 1984),
Witches Brew (Manilla Road, 1985),
The Sorceress (Fates Warning, 1986),
The Conjuring (Megadeth, 1986),
Cry Little Sister (Gerard McMahon, 1987),
By the Grace of the Witch (Savatage, 1988),
Moonchild (Iron Maiden, 1988),
White Witch (Savatage, 1987),
Kiss of Death (Warlock, 1987, "By the light of the moon, I feel a strange desire. By the Light of the Moon I hear the devil's choir. 'Oh, I am," I said, "The queen of the dead..."),
Witches' Dance (Mercyful Fate, 1994),
Bells, Books, and Candles (Graeme Revell, 1996),
If You Ever Did Believe (Stevie Nicks, 1998),
19 Witches (Monster Magnet, 1998), "...you're what you say you are..."
Voodoo (Godsmack, 1999),
Small Town Witch (Sneaker Pimps, 2002),
Special Death (Mirah, 2002),

Big Black Witchcraft Rock (The Cramps, 2003),
Wicked Old Witch (John Fogerty, 2004),
Beloved Enchantress (The Moon and the Nightspirit, 2005),
Burn the Witch (Queens of the Stone Age, 2005),
Witchcraft (Wolfmother, 2005),
American Witch (Rob Zombie, 2006),
Witch's Rune (S. J. Tucker, 2007),
Witch's Wand (Sloan, 2008),
Waking the Witch (Kate Bush, 2008),
Almost anything by Morgana LeFay,
Witch (The Bird and the Bee, 2009),
All of Them Witches (3 Inches of Blood, 2009),
Howl (Florence and the Machine, 2009),
Tres Brujas (The Sword, 2010),
She's My Witch (The Radiacs, 2010),
Witches' Brew (Katy B, 2011),
Nearly Witches (Panic! At the Disco, 2011),
Hex (Neko Case, 2012),
Black Magic (Magic Wands, 2012),
Belispeak (Purity Ring, 2012),
Snow Witch (Huntress, 2012),
Song of the Witches (S. J. Tucker, 2013),
Me and the Devil (Soap&Skin, 2013),
Burning Witches (Black Widow, 2015),
Carrion Flowers (Chelsea Wolfe, 2015),
Black Magic (Little Mix, 2015),
Which Witch (Florence and the Machine, 2015),
Sylvan (Esben and the Witch, 2016),
The Witch (Mark Pickerel, 2016),
Burn the Witch (Radiohead, 2016),
Full Moon Tonight (Silvastone, 2017),
Red Trails (Fever Ray, 2017),

The Witch is Back (Crystal Viper, 2017),
Wild Woman (Sleep Machine, 2017),
Sorcererz (Gorillaz, 2018),
A Little Wicked (Valerie Broussard, 2019),
Witches Mark (King Witch, 2020),
Water Witch (The Secret Sisters, 2020),
Witches (Alice Phoebe Lou, 2020),
The Circle of Five (Burning Witch, 2021),
The Witch of the North (Burning Witches, 2021),
W.I.T.C.H. (Devon Cole, 2023),
Same Old Energy (Kiki Rockwell, 2023)
Ballad of the Witches' Road (from Agatha All Along, 2024)

Some Witchy Travel Suggestions

*This list is also by no means complete. To add experiences and memorials, feel free to contact me at my website: https://www.KerryEBBlack.com

Europe

Scotland has erected many memorials:

The Scottish Witch Trial Museum in Leven, Fife, Scotland

Witch's Well, Edinburg, Scotland

Gallow Green and Maxwelton, Paisley, Scotland (and there's a fun alien gargoyle closeby, too)

Carriden Stone with "witches stone" carved into it, Scotland

Beautiful Statue at Prestonpans, East Lothian, Scotland commemorating the death of 81 people

Culross Plaque and the Valleyfield Wood Plaque (dedicated to Lilias Adie - 1704) in Fife, Scotland (where an estimated 380 people were accused of witchcraft)

Witches Beech Maze, Tullibole Castle, Crook of Devon, Scotland

Maggie Wall Monument, Dunning, Perthshire, Scotland, who may or may not be a real person.

Witch Memorial Plaque at Kirkwell, Orkney commemorates 19 women and 1 man killed 1594-1645

Witches Stone at Forres which states that victims were rolled in barrels studded with spikes from atop Cluny Hill, and then their mangled bodies were burned. This marks the spot of one such burning.

Gallus Quines and Deeds Not Words Street Art in Aberdeen, next to the St. Nicholas Church which was used to imprison suspected witches in 1597. 30 were executed.

Forfar Witch Memorial in Forfar has 22 dots to represent the victims.

Grissel Jaffray Mosaic in Dundee.

Witch's Stone at Monzie, Crieff, for Kate McNieen, who may or may not be a real healer who could turn into a bee.

Witch's Stone at Dornoch honors Janet Horne, an elderly, demented woman tarred, and burned alive in either 1722 or 1727

Cave of the Zugarramurdi, Basque Country (especially the festival at Midsummer

The Museum of Witchcraft and Magic, Bocastle, England

The Chalice Well, Glastonbury, England (Summer Solstice, esp)

Stonehenge, Wiltshire, England

Janua Strega Museum, Benevento, Italy

Museo di Triora Etnografico e della Stegoneria, Triora, Italy (and the annual witches' festival in August)

Harz Mountain Region, Germany, including the Hexentanzplatz sculpture gardens

Hexenturm, Heidelberg, Germany (Witches' Tower)

Hexenturm, Fulda, Germany

Hexenbürgermeisterhaus, museum, Lemgo, Germany

Grimburg Castle and Witch Museum, Hunsruck, Germany

Hexen Hugel, Winningen, Winningen, Germany (stone obelisk carved with names of the twenty victims executed on the site. One of Germany's earliest witch trial memorials.)

Zeiler Stadtturm mit Dokumentationszentrum Hexen, Zeil am Main, Germany (museum)

Wolfshager Hexenbrut (Performing arts group) Langelsheim, Germany

Burg Hohenwerfen (museum in a medieval castle) Austria

Steilneset Witch Trial Memorial, Vardo, Norway

The Museum of Sorcery and Witchcraft, Holmavik, Iceland

The Americas

Salem, Massachusetts boasts a park dedicated in 1992, a memorial at Proctor's Ledge (at the base of the hill where the 19 victims were hung), cemeteries, the "Witch's House," museums, and more. (Plus, you must check out the House of Seven Gables and the Hawthorne House - with a nearby statue of Nathaniel Hawthorne) And there are sites from films, including *Hocus Pocus*. USA

Danvers, Massachusetts (formerly Salem Village) erected a memorial to the trials in 1992 and is home to the Rebecca Nurse Homestead and a recreated meeting house. USA

The Medieval Torture Museum, St. Augustine, Florida, USA

Aquatorium Annual Witch Festival, Octobers in Monongahela, Pennsylvania, USA

Old Dutch Church and Cemetery, Witches' Paddle (October event) in Sleepy Hollow, New York, USA, (& home of the Headless Horseman)

Above Ground Cemeteries tours, and magic and voodoo shops in New Orleans, Louisiana, USA

Buckland Museum of Witchcraft, Cleveland, Ohio, USA

Museum of Anthropology, the Witches' Markets, and the pyramids, Mexico City, Mexico

Lima, Peru La Paz, Mercado de los Brujas (Witches' Market) beneath Gamarra Station

Machu Picchu, Cuzko, Peru

Acknowledgements

As always, I'm eternally grateful to my angel of editing, Debra Sanchez, the brilliant brain and healing heart of Tree Shadow Press. Her guidance and assistance are more magical than I could have hoped for and something for which I am thankful every day. Without her, I wouldn't be the writer I am today. Thank you, Deb, for spreading such enchantment in this crazy world.

Along those lines, I'm blessed by my family. My supportive spouse and the two kiddos still at home allow me to wander through my imagination and encourage me, as well. They pause to listen to a passage with which I've struggled and offer advice. Thank you, darlings. I love you.

And you, dear reader. Thank you for reading this collection of poetry and poetic essays and for sharing my enthusiasm. A story begins in a writer's imagination, but it is realized in the reader's. You picked my book from the millions available to you, and that is a magic all its own!

Please, if you enjoyed this collection of wronged women, bewitching babes, and inspiring enchantresses, spread the word. If you write a review

- or even a few words! - on any of the available platforms (such as Amazon, Bookbub, Goodreads, Fable, etc...), it will boost my book's visibility, which is another magical way to contribute to its success. (And if you do, a billion thank you's!)

Additionally, some of the poems and essays in this collection have been previously published thus:

"Accidental Witchcraft" was published in *Poetic Nightmares*, 2023.
"Poison" was performed by the author on Instagram, June, 2025.
"Witches Conjure" was published in *Death Wish Poetry, Resurrection*, May, 2025.

About the author

Kerry E.B. Black lives in a little, buttercream cottage slipping into a swamp along the Allegheny River outside the city of Steel and Zombies with her sarcastic spouse, two of her five children (the rest have grown and flown to lead interesting lives on their own), a cat named Poe and one named Hemingway, and her little Bear's sweet service dog. When not writing, this member of the Horror Writers' Association (HWA), Nomadic Wordsters, and Wily Writers sings of seniors, advocates for the disabled, travels whenever possible, and reads (and reviews) all she can.

For the newest information about what is yet to be written or where she'll next appear, she invites you to please join her at
https://www.KerryEBBlack.com

And follow on:
Instagram
Blue Sky
You Tube
Facebook
Goodreads
Hive
What once was Twitter

Other works by the author

***Wolves at Bay* is a pseudo-historical novella about family bonds, healing, wolves - both literal and metaphorical - and witchcraft allegations. (Also available in Spanish *Lobos Aulladores*)
***Poetic Nightmares* is a TAZ-nominated collection of horror poetry inspired by the seasons.
***Herd of Nightmares* is Black's TAZ Award winning collection of short scares, flashes of fright, and horror haiku.
***Carousel of Nightmares* is a collection of spooky shorts written with younger readers in mind.
***Fairy Herds and Mythscapes* explores fairy tales and myths through short stories and flash fiction.
***Nightmares on Holidays* guides readers through a calendar year of holiday-themed short stories and flash fiction.
***Awakening at Equinox*, Kerry E.B. Black's debut novel, follows the complicated life of Casey as she and friends attend an autumn ceremony on campus designed to awaken their inner potentials, but they may have awakened something much more sinister. (Also available in Spanish *Despertar En Equinoccio.*)
***Spring of Spirits*, a stand-alone book two in the Seasons of Growing series, continues Casey's adventures. (Also available in Spanish *Primavera de Espíritus.*)

About the Artist

Christopher Robert Blickenderfer was born with a pen in his tight-fisted grip, screaming for artistic expression with his first breath. The owner and lead artist at American Tattoo in Verona, Pennsylvania, USA, Chris's work has earned notice at every stage of his career in many formats, from tattoos to oils, pen and ink, watercolors, and more. Hand Chris a piece of chalk, and doubtless, he'll create a world on a sidewalk. Here are some other covers he has created for Tree Shadow Press:

www.ingramcontent.com/pod-product-compliance
Lightning Source LLC
LaVergne TN
LVHW010049110826
845155LV00028B/264

* 9 7 8 1 9 4 8 8 9 4 4 9 4 *